MOTORCYCLE MESSENGERS 2

TALES FROM THE ROAD BY WRITERS WHO RIDE

Edited by Jeremy Kroeker
Foreword by Charley Boorman

Copyright © 2018 by Oscillator Press. All rights reserved.

All stories, articles, and excerpts are copyright of their creators, and are reproduced here with permission.

The use of any part of this publication reproduced, transmitted in any form or by any means, electronic, mechanical, photo-copying, recording, or otherwise, or stored in a retrieval system, without the prior written consent of the publisher—or, in case of photocopying or other reprographic copying, a license from the Canadian Copyright Licensing Agency—is an infringement of copyright law.

In summary, just buy stuff instead of ripping it off. It really helps actual people.

Library and Archives Canada Cataloguing in Publication

Motorcycle Messengers 2: tales from the road by writers who ride / edited by Jeremy Kroeker

ISBN 978-0-9918250-2-8

Photos by Rosie Gabrielle (YouTube.com/rosiegabrielle)
Cover by Scott Manktelow Design
Editor: Jeremy Kroeker
Copy Editor: Jennifer Groundwater

Printed and bound in Canada

Oscillator Press
368, 160 Kananaskis Way
Canmore, Alberta
T1W 3E2 Canada

OscillatorPress.com

Books by Jeremy Kroeker

Motorcycle Therapy
Through Dust and Darkness

For Bryan Bayley,
ringmaster in his own circus.

Editor's note:

The contributors in this book come from all over the place, and they use different rules for spelling and grammar. During the editing process, we've tried to be consistent with style while respecting individual preferences. (We did use Canadian punctuation conventions). If there is an error, the blame falls on Oscillator Press, not the author.

If you're into adventure, we think you'll love this book.
But if you're also a spelling enthusiast, it might drive you bananas.

It nearly drove us bananas putting it together.

FOREWORD

By Charley Boorman

Travel is in my blood. For sure, I had an unusual upbringing being the child of an up-and-coming film director. My father's career meant we as a family were in a perpetual orbit around the world, from movie set to movie set. One month, we'd be in the southern states of the USA filming *Deliverance*, and then we'd find ourselves in the Brazilian rainforest filming *The Emerald Forest*. My father, John Boorman, was the inspiration that firmly embedded the wanderlust gene into my body and soul, while our Irish home in County Wicklow brought me down to earth and gave me some roots to hang on to.

Throughout my life's journey, travel books have urged me on to further adventures of my own. Over the years, I've increasingly turned to audio books. I just love riding the big distances with a cracking tale of adventure in my headphones.

Some of the great travel writers have mastered a way to describe a scene. You're taken there, transported into that moment to share that same experience. These authors have inspired me not only to travel but to write, record, and share those moments in time. I am without doubt indebted to them. They helped shape my view of the world and enabled me to dream about wider horizons.

I hope you all have at least a section of bookshelf at home where you have your travel and adventure collection. (I certainly do. I like to pick not just by author, but by continent or country.)

Having read all the "must-reads," you can search further afield and find some little-known gems. When I was riding across Australia's outback with my good mate, Billy Ward, we met a cool old wrinkly guy in the Outback. He was a great raconteur and after a couple of beers he began to tell us about an historic, little-known Australian adventurer.

This very special man, Frank Birtles, pedalled his way into the dead heart of the country, a place so hot and dry they called it "the oven." This was in the late 1800s and early 1900s. He'd just jump on his pedal bike and ride for thousands of kilometres into the unknown, with no idea where he'd get water from (one of the biggest challenges, of course), and with no hope of help. He became a real pioneer. Not many people seem to have heard of him, yet what he accomplished was incredible. Since chatting to the old guy in Broken Hill, I have bought the book—it's a great read.

Today we live in a world that often drains our opportunity and our motivation to take that leap of faith. We have busy jobs and families, mortgages, and school plays to attend. I know it's not easy to make that adventure happen. But an adventure doesn't mean you have to be that pioneer, like Frank Birtles. The adventure is *your* adventure, something that challenges you a lot or even just a bit.

You don't have to ride around the world, the Simpson Desert, Antarctica, or Death Valley. My message is about having a go—about trying new things, about taking a chance. What I've learnt from the likes of Ted Simon and others is that the journey itself is the adventure. Failure doesn't matter. The problems, the break-downs—both mechanical and personal—are often magical keys that can unlock doors to incredible personal experiences.

The journey underway, we can temporarily put modern constraints like work, mortgage, bills, and gloomy TV news behind us. We begin to find out who we truly are. We experience the luxury of a level of self-discovery.

In this anthology from Jeremy, rider-authors have grasped their own opportunities. Gone out on limbs, taken chances. Through good and bad times, each has had an amazing adventure and lived to tell the tale.

Let this book of adventure tales proposition you to open your mind to the endless possibilities that life—our own personal unique *adventure*—can present to each and every one of us.

Charley Boorman 2018

STORIES

ALONE IN THE JUNGLE: RIDING THE REAL HO CHI MINH TRAIL

By Antonia Bolingbroke-Kent

Fuelled by fear and pounded by rain, I squelched and slipped through the deserted forest. For the first time in my life, death felt a possibility: a stupid, pointless, lonely end on the aptly named Mondulkiri Death Highway. I cursed myself for being so stubborn and stupid, for ignoring the warnings, for being so obsessive about following the Ho Chi Minh Trail. If I did die, it would be death by hubris, my own stupid fault. My only hope was to keep walking. But for how long, I could only guess.

Five weeks earlier, I'd wobbled through the Hanoi traffic, my pink Honda Cub a mere dot in the barging torrent of man and machine. For the next six weeks, I'd be following the Ho Chi Minh Trail; a legendary transport network which had once spread 12,000 miles through Vietnam, Laos, and Cambodia. The means by which Uncle Ho's communist North was able to send men and supplies to defeat the American-backed South, the Trail had been the fulcrum of the Vietnam War. I'd first encountered the Trail whilst working on a BBC documentary the previous year, and was soon hooked. Before the shoot was over, I knew I wanted to come back, alone, to explore what remained of this once mighty web before time, nature, and development swallowed it forever.

Aided by *Top Gear's* 2008 Vietnam special, biking has surged in popularity in Vietnam. But while scores of travellers ride a tourist-friendly, tarmac version of the Trail between Hanoi and Ho Chi Minh City, only a handful follow its gnarly guts over the Truong Son Mountains into Laos. Even fewer trace it south into the wild eastern reaches of Cambodia. I wanted to do both. Unlike the hundreds of thousands of North Vietnamese who walked, drove, and worked on the Trail in the sixties and seventies, I wouldn't have to deal with a daily deluge of bombs. But UXO—unexploded ordnance—littered my route south; cerebral malaria, dengue fever, and dysentery were still prevalent; and the trees slithered and crawled with unpleasant creatures.

Despite these dangers, I was intent on riding alone, on stripping away the protective blanket of companionship to see what I was really made of. How would I react when my bike ground to a halt in the middle of a river? Could I hack days and nights alone in the jungle? Only through the purity of solitude would I find the answers.

I also never had any doubt about the choice of bike. With three gears, an automatic clutch, slender city wheels, and brakes that would barely stop a bolting snail, the Honda Cub isn't the most obvious off-roader. But with my meagre budget and limited mechanical know-how, the cheap, idiot-proof bike suited me perfectly. Sourced and pimped for me by Hanoi motorbike tour company Explore Indochina, my 85cc model cost a mere $350.

Vietnam was Trail-lite, a gentle introduction to what lay ahead. My bike, which I dubbed The Pink Panther, spun along the smooth tarmac of the Ho Chi Minh Highway and roadside cafes, where fuel and cheap hotels were in abundance. In a nation of 90 million people, I was rarely alone. Everywhere I stopped, curious crowds gathered around me, firing me with friendly questions. Where was I from? Where was I going? Where was my husband? Why was I alone? Never has a phrasebook been so thoroughly thumbed.

At times the Vietnamese were a little too friendly. Twice in the first week, as I sat slurping noodle soup at a roadside shack, men approached and offered me 500,000 dong—$23—for a lunch-time quickie. I wasn't sure if it was the pink bike, the fact that I was a lone western female, or the irresistible cocktail of the two. Sweaty, devoid of make-up, and dressed in biker gear, I couldn't see the appeal.

Aside from a few dull, misty days south of Hanoi, the scenery was fantastic, alternating between cascading rice paddies, banana plantations, sugar cane fields, and patches of verdant forest. Dawdling along at 20 miles per hour, I drank in this Otherness: men in pith helmets—a hangover from years of war—led sullen water buffaloes along the verge; scores of ancient Honda Cubs chuntered along, obscured under titanic loads; farmers tended to their paddies, hinged at the waist like compasses; and everywhere men and women chopped and loaded newly harvested sugar cane, piling it onto waiting buffalo carts. It wasn't long before my initial nerves dissipated, replaced by the soaring elation one only gets from the open road. Already I didn't want this journey to end.

After a week I reached the Mu Gia pass, a narrow conduit through the wall of the Truong Son that had served as North Vietnam's principal route to the Trail in Laos. Blasted by US bombs and defoliants, nowadays the 418-metre pass is a quiet border crossing little used by westerners. I'd been warned that I'd never make it across, that the Lao border guards were known for turning back foreigners, that I'd have to make a lengthy diversion to a more tourist-friendly crossing. But I was determined to try.

Miraculously, I made it through the Rubik's Cube of Vietnamese and Lao customs and was soon standing on the other side of the pass, admiring the new world before me. And what a new world it was. It was as if the mountains were the heavy velvet curtain of a theatre, drawn back to reveal a wholly different reality. Only six hours earlier I had ridden through a drizzly Vietnamese dawn, my fleece and Weise motorbike jacket zipped up against the cold. Now I stood in a thin cotton shirt, pounded by forty-degree heat, the empty, karst-rimmed valley below me shimmering in the noon inferno. Laos, the hot, sparsely populated crucible of the Trail, was going to be very different.

The following morning I rode south through a Lost World landscape of tinder-dry jungle and pinnacles of slate-grey karst. Panther's tyres, which I'd let down a few bar to help with the dirt, crunched over red laterite, sending clouds of dust billowing about me. Formerly a main north-south artery of the Trail, the road-side was punctured with bomb craters, a reminder of the USAF's extreme efforts to destroy the Trail. Between 1965 and 1973,

2,093,100 tonnes of ordnance were dropped on this neutral country; an onslaught which gave Laos the deadly accolade of being the most-bombed country per capita on earth, a title it retains to this day.

Many of these bombs still remain, as I was reminded that afternoon when foolishly walking through the scrub in search of an old Vietnamese anti-aircraft gun emplacement. In a pile of leaves inches from the path lay a single cluster bomb. One wrong step and this tennis-ball-sized killer would have blown me to bits.

Most of the scattered villages I rode through were home to Laos' animist tribal minorities, who make up 40 per cent of the country's 6.3 million people. They were simple bamboo and wood affairs with no sanitation or electricity and few schools. Poor subsistence farmers, many of these people had rarely—if ever—seen foreigners before. As I passed through, scattering oinking black piglets and scrawny chickens, some of the ragged children ran after me, waving and shouting "Sabaidee!" Others simply froze and stared, open-mouthed. Several groups of women ran away, hitching up their sarongs and bolting into the forest like deer startled by a wolf. Nowhere else in the world has this ever happened to me. It was most odd.

Everywhere, there were reminders of the war. Stilted huts were built on cluster-bomb casings, boys paddled in canoes made from discarded aeroplane fuel canisters, and cows wore bells fashioned from old mortar fuses. In one village, Ban Phanop, the wing of a crashed US F-4 fighter leaned against a tree and two live

500-pound bombs lay under a family's hut, waiting to be sold for scrap metal. Farther south, around the old Trail command post at La Hap, I rode down an eerie, dark track flanked by craters, past the rusted, bombed-out remains of North Vietnamese trucks.

In this remote, inaccessible region, accommodation options were limited. I spent most nights in government-run guesthouses-cum-brothels—grim establishments seeping with leprous patches of damp. Food was equally basic and I subsisted on a diet of sticky rice, eggs, peanut brittle, warm Coca-Cola, Beerlao, and gritty black Vietnamese coffee laced with dollops of condensed milk.

But I hadn't come for Egyptian cotton and Cordon Bleu cuisine, and the tough, exhilarating riding more than made up for it. One day I'd be sliding down sun-dappled jungle tracks, my wheels spinning through lakes of orange mud; the next I'd be struggling up steep ladders of basalt, yelping like a Soviet weightlifter as I heaved and paddled the bike upwards. I bumped over original Trail cobblestones, sliced through deep white sand, buzzed across parched grass plateaus dotted with pines, and spun along graded red dirt in obliterating veils of dust. Some days I'd creep forward, metre by metre, brakes squealing, engine straining, sweat trickling down my spine. By the time I reached each grotty guesthouse I was caked in a carapace of mud and dust, drenched in sweat, famished, and in dire need of a Beerlao. I wouldn't have wanted to be anywhere else.

The manifold rivers dissecting the Truong Son region were another obstacle. Generally it was a case of throttle-on-feet-up-and-ride, hoping the engine wouldn't conk out or I'd get an ignominious ducking. Other crossings were more perilous, such as having to balance on a terrifyingly narrow, wobbly canoe as a toothless old man pushed me across with a single pole. On one occasion Panther was carried across by a gaggle of glistening, nut-brown children.

There were few people and little other traffic. Barring the odd moped and tuk-tuk—prehistoric-looking tractor-trailer hybrids common in Southeast Asia—I had the roads to myself.

Panther was less delighted with the task at hand. A few weeks in she began sounding like a bronchitic tractor and in Kaleum, a small town on the soon-to-be-dammed Sekong River, she refused to start at all. A chain-smoking, tattooed Vietnamese mechanic quickly diagnosed the problem: the cam chain and sprockets had gone, in turn damaging the valves and cylinder barrel. The next day, after a $40 engine rebuild, we were back in action. But by the time I reached Cambodia, the incident had been repeated twice. It was hard to fathom why the same thing kept happening over and over again. It could have been due to poor-quality parts, or each mechanic setting the cam timing wrong. Or maybe it was simply that Panther couldn't cope with the Ho Chi Minh Trail.

The border was quick and easy and soon I was riding south along the tarmac of Highway 13 into the heat-scorched Mekong lowlands of Cambodia. On either side were the same red earth and stilted houses as Laos; only the billboards advertising Khmer beers and the upcoming elections spoke of a new country. It's funny how we always want what we don't have. There were times in Laos when I would have given my last dime for a sliver of tarmac. But in the next few days, as I buzzed along new Chinese-built highways through miles and miles of rubber plantations, I craved the mountains and jungle I'd left behind.

I also missed the Trail. From scant references in books and a few clues on my old Vietnamese Trail map, I knew that it had fingered its way through the jungles of northeast Cambodia. But time, civil war, and the genocidal Khmer Rouge had largely wiped it from existence and memory, and clues were thin on the ground. Even hiring a (rather grumpy) translator in Ban Lung for a few days threw little light on the matter. Riding east through banana, rubber, and cashew plantations and illegally logged jungle, we asked numerous village elders if they knew anything of the Trail. Myopic Jarai chiefs whose huts were perched between multiple bomb craters shook their heads. A skeletal old man living in Ba Kham, a crater-pocked village marked as a supply base on the old map, eyed me suspiciously and denied all knowledge. Even if they could remember, I realised they weren't going to tell me. Persecuted by Pol Pot and looked down upon by the lowlands Khmers, Ratanakiri's tribal minorities had rarely come off well from contact with questioning outsiders.

South of Lumphat lay the Mondulkiri Death Highway, a ninety-mile dirt track through uninhabited forest soon to be upgraded by the Chinese. The *Lonely Planet* warned it should only be attempted in dry season by "hardcore bikers" with "years of experience and an iron backside." However, since the only other way south was a three-hundred-mile diversion back via the Mekong, it didn't occur to me not to attempt it. Panther and I had survived Laos; surely there was nothing we couldn't tackle now.

But early rains had churned the surface into a morass of lakes, ruts, and bogs through which I splashed, struggled, and heaved, my legs swallowed by the sticky slime. Stubbornly I persisted. I was averaging little more than walking pace, but if I kept buggering on, metre by metre, minute by minute, I'd make it to the first town in Mondulkiri before nightfall. Even when the only human I saw—a young man on a moped with two dead cockerels strung over his handlebars—stopped and motioned for me not to go on, I ignored his advice and ploughed on anyway. If you listened to everyone in life who told you not to go on you would never get anywhere, I thought. He might well be right, but I had to see for myself.

He was right: as dusk fell, Panther sank in the mire for the umpteenth time that day, but now not even the brute force of fear could move her. Suddenly the situation seemed critical. Without help, it was impossible for me to haul her out. But I was alone in the jungle and very low on water. I had no choice but to leave her and walk for help.

If it hadn't been for a Cambodian road workers' camp I stumbled into hours later, dangerously dehydrated and partially delirious, things could have been very different. I'll never forget those kind men who took me in, fed me rice and water, and helped me retrieve the bike the following morning. No longer starting, I got her trucked the 30 miles to Ban Lung, where she had her fourth engine rebuild.

As the young Vietnamese guards stamped me back into their country, Ho Chi Minh City was only 150 miles south. So near the end, my emotions returned to the see-sawing unpredictability of the first few days. Weeks of hard riding, extreme heat, poor diet, and lack of sleep were chipping away at my energy levels and I knew it was time to finish. But following the Trail had been thrilling, engrossing, poignant, and ceaselessly compelling. I didn't want it to end.

Babbling with nerves and excitement, I buzzed towards Ho Chi Minh City through a panorama of mirror-flat paddies and drooping palms. Teenage girls bicycled in giggling groups; wooden carts pulled by handsome conker-brown oxen trundled along the verge; and swarms of mopeds carried families, trussed-up pigs, and cages of cowering dogs. Through the middle lurched overcrowded buses and hooting KAMAZ trucks, none of which slowed for anything or anyone. Riding at 15 miles per hour, I watched the road and my mirrors obsessively, keen to avoid a last-minute accident.

Gradually the buildings became taller, the palms disappeared, and the traffic swelled to a raging flood. Everywhere there was traffic, mopeds, engine noise, and masked faces under multi-coloured helmets. I was in Ho Chi Minh City. At last, the Reunification Palace, my final destination, loomed ahead.

"We've made it, Panther," I said out loud, as my wheels touched the gates. "We've bloody made it."

A group of Japanese tourists stopped photographing the palace and looked at me.

I couldn't believe we'd actually done it. For ten minutes I just sat there, staring at the white façade, smiling, savouring the moment. Six weeks, three countries, two thousand miles, four engine rebuilds, and one hell of an adventure later, my Ho Chi Mission was finally over.

Antonia Bolingbroke-Kent is a British author, TV producer and expedition leader with a particular penchant for solo journeys through remote regions.

Her globetrotting began in 2006, when she and a friend drove a bright pink tuk-tuk a record-breaking 12,561 miles from Bangkok to Brighton, raising £50,000 for the mental health charity Mind in the process. Following the trip, Antonia penned her first book, Tuk Tuk to the Road.

After a bonkers few years producing TV shows and organizing extreme charity adventures in Mongolia, Cameroon and Siberia, in 2013 she set off on her first major solo trip, a two-month exploration of Indochina's legendary Ho Chi Minh Trail on a vintage pink Honda Cub. It was a journey that involved copious amounts of mud, multiple breakdowns, and a few very near misses. The resulting book, A Short Ride in the Jungle, *was* Overland *magazine's Book of the Year.*

In 2016 Antonia embarked on another solo expedition, this time across the remote, mountainous Northeast Indian state of Arunachal Pradesh. The book she wrote about this journey, Land of the

Dawn-Lit Mountains, *was shortlisted for the Stanford's Adventure Travel Book of the Year.*

When she's not writing or travelling, Antonia lives in Bristol with her boyfriend Marley. Together they run www.edge-expeditions.com.

🌐 *TheItinerant.co.uk*

🐦 *@AntsBK*

📷 *@AntsBK*

BE NICE TO HIPPOS

By Billy Ward

Karma is just around the next bend—honest.

Having badly failed the audition for Fifty Shades
of Grey—The Musical, *Billy heads back to southern
Africa to work through his frustration guiding a
group of riders across southern Africa. Another day
in the life of Billy Biketruck.*

Riding a new BMW 1200 GSA Adventure through rural Zambia in
the summer is such a pleasure and a nice way to spend one's life—
and earn a living. The sun was shining and my spirits were high.
The main group of riders was hours ahead of me now, due to the
fact that I was fulfilling my "Tail-End Charley" role, which means
fixing a few punctures along the way and helping riders through
some challenging sandy sections. Front-End Charley (a.k.a. Charley
Boorman—a proper Charley) was undoubtedly already at the destination hotel and ready to cool off in the pool after sipping an
African favourite, a spiced rum and Coke.

Earlier I'd spent a couple of hours at a collapsed bridge. The fact
that it had collapsed wouldn't have been clear 'til it was too late.
You'd find yourself flying through the air with all the local kids

watching, perhaps thinking you were really cool—'til the landing. Not having Sky Channel or Guy Martin on tap, the local kids get a lot of pleasure watching old white people doing stupid things on big motorbikes in their backyard. It's probably educational, too.

The bridge had washed out during recent biblical rains (apparently sent by someone's God due to a Gay Pride march in San Francisco eight months earlier) and the way across was now down a steep siding into the dry sandy riverbed and back up the other bank. The sand was deep. Deep enough to make you feel like you'd chosen the wrong bike, wrong tyres, wrong body, and wrong holiday. I was unsure whether I was the last rider or not, so I decided to wait for a while and make certain no latecomers inadvertently did an Evel Knievel over the ravine.

I checked my watch. It was about 4:30 in the afternoon and as sunset would be between 5:30 and 6:00, I decided not to wait any longer. I was definitely the last man standing and needed to crack on. Riding in the dark in Africa is a massive big "no"—the nighttime is for the animals. A few miles down the track, I came across Brian and Karen, an Australian couple on a BMW GS 800 with a flat rear tyre, stuck at the side of the track, looking hot and a bit stressed. They'd obviously been there a while.

"Hoorah, Billy's here, our hero," I heard them say—in my head. They may have also said, "He's so cool, clever and attractive. He'll fix the puncture and we can catch up with the rest of the group before the lions, tigers, and bears come out looking for their dinner." Of course, that may have been in my head as well.

The trouble is, when it comes to punctures, the GS 1200s with their tubeless tyres are literally a ten-minute job, but the GS 800s are tubed. It's a different story. Wheel off, tyre off, tube out, etc. I was really only equipped for the quick-fix 1200s, so we had a conundrum: three people, one working bike, it was getting dark and I'm experienced enough to know that lions eat people, elephants trample them, and hippos may be vegetarian, but they're continually angry and can give you a nasty suck.

We were in the bush about a kilometre from a river. It was hot and sticky, with a beautiful yet mysterious canopy of jungle in the near distance where the hungry bad things live. We had no phone cover and no chance of getting help and were at least four hours' ride away from any form of civilisation. I had to work through the possible solutions quickly.

Brian was a nice guy. His wife Karen was gorgeous. Okay, I had it. Send Brian on ahead on my bike, while I created a Bear-Grylls-inspired night shelter for Karen and me. It would be a cold night, but using our own body heat wisely, we'd probably make it through. Brian could organise our recovery in the morning, or in a few days, or weeks. Okay, okay—so I was lonely.

While I was still musing through my options, Brian grabbed my arm. "Billy, the sun is dropping below the horizon. This is serious, man, what are we going to do?"

So, the right course of action was taken. Working on the karma principle and the simple fact that it was my job to look after the clients, I gave them my bike and wished them a safe onward journey to the comfort and safety of the hotel, some four or five hours' ride away. I'd stay the night there with their bike and they could arrange the support vehicle to return early in the morning with a few tools and an inner tube. Don't you just hate reality sometimes?

As the loving couple rode off into the setting sun, clutching each other tightly, I waved, gently wiping a tear from my eye and wondering which was worse: being eaten alive by a lion or buggered by a hippo in the dead of night. Yes, I know, I'm a bit of a thinker.

I moved the bike into the bush and went collecting wood and stones to create the centrepiece of my evening—a fire. This would be a bad time to get bitten by a snake, so I sang ABBA songs really loudly as I moved through the scrub, searching for fuel. Snakes hate ABBA; it's a commonly known fact.

Twilight here is really non-existent and in a very short time the sun had gone to bed and the stars were twinkling across a beautiful black canopy. The Milky Way was as clear as in an astronomy textbook. I'd built a nice camp with branches, some big logs, and stones. I'd used some petrol-soaked rags wrapped around a couple of sticks as a way to scare animals away in an emergency and placed them to one side, like in the movies. I also had a collection of rocks; my handy catapult, bought in Lusaka from a ten-year-old; a Swiss Army knife; and my military strike torch, all neatly laid out in my armoury in case the bad things came to get me.

I had good night vision and felt pretty happy in my little wilderness camp—'til I lit the fire, that is. Then my vision was restricted to the immediate area around the fire. Looking outward to the bush, it was just pitch-black, full of demons' eyes, lions and tigers—all of them staring back at me and waiting.

In those few seconds, I changed from "Billy Big-Bollox" to wanting my mummy now. Right now!

Being a little dismayed at how quick my wood pile was being consumed by the raging bonfire, I acknowledged the stark reality that at some point I'd need to venture back into the bush for more wood. Re-reading my survival leaflet, which conveniently came free with my Swiss Army knife, I noted that neither lion attacks nor hippo-buggerings were covered in any great detail. I could feel the change in the air as the hot, sticky sweat of the day was now having a chilling effect on my meaty, edible, and desirable body. That's when the noises started.

At first it was just an occasional hooting owl and a snorting pig-like noise. Then came the frogs, bats, and insects. A veritable orchestra of fauna began to ring out in every direction. I tried to keep calm and roll with it. I've heard it all before—but not alone, in the dark, in the bush. It wasn't easy. It sounded so much nicer whilst sipping a cocktail on the veranda at the Victoria Falls Hotel.

Then just when I thought I was good, my nerves were shattered by a crunching, munching, rushing noise that clearly indicated something large nearby. This was underpinned by a deep, breathy baritone grunting that caused nearby bushes to resonate and birds to take flight.

Hippos make a great noise. Once you've heard it, you'll always recognise it. Their mouths can open as wide as two metres from top to bottom jaw—which, when you think about it, means that I could literally stand up inside a hippo's mouth. Their teeth are sharp and full of bacteria, and a bull can weigh in at over three tons. It's as big as a small van—a van with teeth, bad breath, and a wicked temper.

Well, I knew what it was and I was scared, for sure. Hippos can often travel a few miles from the river in search of good grass. I looked around my camp and noticed how lovely the grass seemed. Then, a long way away I heard what was definitely a kill—that desperate throaty scream and gurgle of a poor creature that was obviously now in the mouth of a predator.

At least this took my mind off the hippo.

Out of sheer terror, I considered running along the road in the direction of the hotel, just to be out of the bush—but funnily enough, prey animals do this too, for the same reasons. And predators sit in wait at the side of the road—just like it's a sushi-bar conveyor belt—so I dropped that idea. Nope, there was nowhere to run. I even thought of praying, but was unsure to whom—so many gods these days.

I kept sitting in the light of the fire; my ears were like radar. I noticed how the noises changed throughout the night as different cycles of life moved on or stopped. I thought, ironically, how lucky I was to even experience these fears and my mind took me back to living on a scruffy housing estate in Liverpool as a teenager, with high unemployment, high crime, and limited horizons.

I thought, too, how my eight-year-old had told her class and teacher a few years ago that her dad was an adventurer, like the man in the Indiana Jones films, and how I was invited to do a talk about Africa to the rest of the school. So, all in all things were good, yeah?

The noises morphed into a low background melody. I'd not been eaten yet and I slowly drifted off into deeper thoughts and memories about success and failure, about relationships, nasal hair, and the merits of waxing. If I did get eaten right now, would I have changed anything that had gone before?

"Billy, Billy...! What are you on?" came a voice, driving a thin wedge between my dreams and reality. It took a second or two to break away from my thoughts and then I saw John, our lead guide, a Cyclops with his military-style head torch casting a beam of diffused red light across my camp. He was walking towards me, his body framed majestically by a glowing sky: the beginnings of a new dawn.

The fire was out, but still smoldering. Apparently, John had been looking for me for a good hour or so.

"Bet you were shitting yourself out here, Billy boy!" He said as we loaded the stricken BMW onto the trailer.

"Nah, not really, John," I said, full of confidence "Hard-core mate, all good here. Just another day in the office."

Stay happy, take opportunities, and be nice to hippos...

Adventure motorcyclist, presenter, speaker, producer, journalist, and all-round "good egg" Billy Ward travels extensively with TV personalities like Charley Boorman and Ross Noble. He counts global hotspots among his travel destinations—Iraq and Afghanistan, for example—and has a strong affinity for the continent of Africa, where he trained to become a registered Safari Guide. In the realm of television and media, Billy is comfortable working at both ends of the camera. With his lightning-white hair, a hankering for adrenalin-riddled adventure, and a generous portion of humour, Billy has been described has having a "serious dash of Liverpudlian wit, topped off with a dollop of Irish blarney." He's a bloke that talks the talk and walks the walk ... but he can't chew gum.

🌐 *BikeTruck.com*
🐦 *@biketruck*
📘 */biketruck*

TERRA INCOGNITA

By Chris Scott

> *In this adaptation from his* Street Riding Years
> *memoir, adventure motorcycling author Chris Scott*
> *recalls his first teenage motorcycle adventure.*

It was the perfect night for a small accident. For two weeks I'd
been prowling the neighbourhood's avenues on my new moped,
perfecting my moves, exploring the limits. The time had now come
for juvenile confidence to overtake experience.

That chilly winter's night, I was encased in my mountaineering
duvet jacket under a NATO-patterned shooting coat and a pair
of huge AA patrolman's gauntlets. Snugly camouflaged for north
European warfare that was sure to come, I felt invulnerable, if a
little on the hot side. The moment had come to see just what my
Honda SS50 could do. It was time to go for the big Four Zero.

Ahead of me there was no shimmering salt lake, no deserted
runway with paramedics on standby. I was at the summit of a back
street with a fire station down on the corner of the busy Brighton
Road. If the atmospheric friction of hitting Mach 0.0525 saw me
burst into flames, like Steve Austin in the opening sequence of
The Six Million Dollar Man, I was sure the brigade would be on hand
to hose me down. That's if they weren't on strike.

It was January 1977. The previous summer's heat wave had passed, and with it had gone my interest in schooling. A few weeks after dutifully trotting into the sixth form, it dawned on me I didn't have to be there anymore. So I made my excuses, cleared my desk, and strode down the hill singing The Who's "I'm Free," and actually meaning it. My school tie—two halves stapled together and pockmarked with magnifying-glass burns—was scrunched in my pocket, never to be worn again. I felt exhilarated. While it may not have been blown to pieces—for me, on that October day, School—Was—Out—For—Ever.

The Saturday job at the supermarket became full-time and, as I was still living at home, my £20 weekly wage meant that by the new year I could afford not only an alpine duvet jacket and a Chouinard ice axe, but a hundred and twenty quids' worth of moped as well. Looking back, £120 seems extravagant. Was I bike-mad? Not really. At that time, the classic climbing routes of Chamonix held more interest than Brands Hatch or the Isle of Man TT. Barry Sheene may have just become world champion, but I didn't know him from Barry Humphries, nor a Yamaha "Fizzie" from a can of Fanta. Instead, like most sixteen-year-olds, I was bored of pedalling myself around these last ten years and saw motorbikes as a natural progression. I assumed I'd eventually migrate to cars, but right now I was ready for the excitement and adventure of motorbikes. I imagine I'd felt the same when I'd learned to walk fifteen years earlier.

I was a player in the finale of Britain's brief sports moped craze, when a manly, full-power, leg-over mini-motorcycle came with an actual kick-start, actual gears, and a saddle for two—and we all knew what that suggested. Until recently in Europe, the word "moped" had signified 50cc "pedal-and-go" stick insects like Puchs or Mobylettes, with a wire basket on the front and flat-out at 29 miles an hour. Then, responding to the boom, canny manufacturers soon fell over themselves to design the fastest, flashiest, and most furious fifty. Accident rates for under-seventeens went off the graph.

Among these Sixteener Specials, Yamaha's two-stroke FSIE (the "Fizzie") was by far the most popular in the UK and one of the fastest, along with the Italian Fantic 50 and the Garelli. In my last weeks of school, a rich kid had come in on a Garelli Tiger Cross. "Flash bastard," we all muttered. Lucky flash bastard, though. As soon as you got your hands on your two-stroke sports moped, you set about adapting it to scream up to 52 mph, to the intense annoyance of anyone in earshot, giving rise to the cry:

"'Oo does 'e think 'e is, Barry Sheene?'"

Like on the Fizzie, my Honda's engine was suspended from its pressed-steel frame and thrust forward like Bruce Lee's slab-smashing fist. A high-level silencer was clad in a perforated chrome guard to suggest heat, power, and melted PVC overtrousers.

The reason I'd settled on the Honda was that the only person I knew with a sports moped—my ex-schoolmate Phil—let me have a go on his. I wasn't bothered about not getting the fastest fifty because I wasn't going to be riding a moped one minute past my seventeenth birthday, which was only a few months away. At that point I'd get a proper 250cc motorbike. All I needed to do was learn how to ride.

The idea of being taught by experts in a car park full of cones never occurred to me or my mum. Instead, Phil came round and showed me how to spur his SS into life with the kick-starter. The motor ran with a muted purr that was so much more refined than a two-stroke Fizzie's ear-grating din. I turned the throttle and the purring became more insistent. I did it again. Vrrroooom... vroom-vrooooom.

"Yeah, all right, steady on, Chris. You'll bend a valve."

Phil patiently explained the launch procedure. First, pull in the clutch lever on the left handlebar, then click down to select first gear with the left foot. Now the tricky bit: synchronise the release of the clutch with the turning of the throttle on the right 'bar, while balancing and steering. I listened without really taking any of it in.

With my right foot on the ground steadying me, I pulled in the clutch, trod down on the gear lever, and turned the throttle. Then, once the engine was making a good noise, I released the clutch like a bowstring. The little bike shot out from under my legs, ran on, then tipped over and scraped down the road. Wondering what had just happened, I stood there, legs apart and slightly bent, hands resting on handlebars that were no longer there. Phil rushed over to attend to his moped, an instinct ingrained in any biker, as I'd soon learn. No matter how crippled you were, guts spilling down the road, the first thing you did was right the bike and make sure it was okay. Only then was it safe to pass out.

Watching Phil's SS50 catapult away from me, I was beginning to see what they meant by "sports mopeds." These were clearly highly-strung beasts—snarling, petrol-fed leopards that would require some taming. We tried again, and eventually I got the bike to move off with me still on it.

Once I had my own black SS50, mastering the coordination of the controls was child's play. Cornering, braking, and even timing the gear changes with a dip in power delivery were much the same as on pushbikes—and now the night had come to give my onyx leopard its head and see what forty miles per hour felt like.

I set off down the hill, shuffled a little, then hunkered down purposefully, just like those ski jumpers on telly. I was focused not on a jump but on the speedo needle, steadily calibrating a similar leap into the abyss. I had to reach thirty well before halfway—any later and I'd shoot into the heavy traffic of the Brighton Road.

The 2.5 horsepower motor screeched beneath me, aided by the lethal gradient. The needle crept around the dial, 34 mph... 35... into top gear ... 36... 37... 37.5... the junction wasn't so far ahead now. I tucked in a bit more... 38... I'm running out of road... 38.5... The motor screamed. Sod it! I'm not going to make it.

"Houston, I can't hold her. She's breaking up. She's breaking—"

I snatched at the brakes as if I were pruning a gnarly shrub, and the combination of wet road and seventies-era tyres made the bike flip in an instant. The Honda and I slid helplessly down the road towards the junction, until the friction of our assorted extremities slowed us to a stop.

Luckily, my timing was better than my braking technique and we came to rest below the Give Way sign. I'd had my first "prang." In my over-padded get-up I was unharmed, but the Honda's headlamp, indicators and ungainly pedals were never to regain their factory-perfect alignment. Mach 0.0525 would have to wait for another day.

A few weeks earlier the postman had delivered a beautifully produced 32-page brochure showcasing Honda's superb range of motorcycles. In it, each succulent model was allotted a full page comprising a studio photo, technical data in two neat columns, and a colour illustration of you (possibly your lady) and your Honda in an idealised setting. Take the ST70 minibike: it rested by a village pond where Angler Man was hauling in a prize carp. Opposite was the CF70 Chaly, another dinky runabout, but a step-thru and so clearly pitched at the demurer sex. Its setting was a fairground where a coven of playful nymphs clad in miniskirts appeared to be rehearsing their routine. On the next page, the smart CB200 twin was assisting at a hot-air-ballooning event. I'd seen CB200s around, and with their distinctive vinyl tank patches I thought them extremely handsome machines. A few pages on, the CB360K6 watched over two enraptured lovers enjoying a Mediterranean sunset. And who could miss the sensational CB400F? It was featured, cranked over on the front cover, all the better to present its sensuously contoured four-into-one downpipes like a sexed-up baboon.

Below it ran Honda's pithy mission statement: "More Sense, More Style." It summed up my own teenage aspirations.

Even before that brochure arrived, I'd become infatuated with my first motorcycle. It sat in the window of a tiny shop on Mitcham Lane in Streatham, a black and chrome apparition hovering gently behind the glass. Back then it was just One Sexy-Looking Motorbike—a Triumph—but the shiny chrome features have stayed with me: a perforated round air-filter housing and a tank-top grill on which to lash your oilskins. It was probably a mid-sixties T100SS with clip-ons and rear-sets. So my early taste wasn't so bad, even if it was already a decade behind the times. At least it wasn't a Fantic chopper or some horrible 175cc Jawa breadbin.

Before I discovered bikes, I'd taken up rock climbing. Unfortunately, I was living in the wrong end of the country to make the most of that. I'd climbed everything going inside the house and the doorframes were beginning to show the strain. The artificial climbing wall up at the Sobell Sports Centre in Finsbury Park, north London, was the next best thing. With my EB rock shoes stuffed in a knapsack, I undertook my first motorcycling adventure one February evening after work: a bold traverse from Norbury, SW16 to Finsbury Park, N7, to be done *direttissima*, in the spirit of climbing legend Walter Bonatti. From SW16 down to SW1 and all the way back up to N7 would mean covering no less than twenty-three postal zones—something I wasn't sure I could manage without porters and extra oxygen.

I set off up the Brighton Road towards central London to negotiate the bandit-ridden badlands of the Elephant and Castle,
then forded the swiftly flowing River Thames by means of the
Blackfriars Bridge. Beyond lay terra incognita, a mysterious region
which the most recent maps identified as "north London." I buzzed
warily over Ludgate Circus and below the ornate Holborn Viaduct.
Just beyond, Topham Street, EC1 remains ingrained in my memory
as the very first time I breathlessly matched an actual street name
with the index and page of an A-Z street atlas—"ground to map,"
as aged navigators call it. With my position reaffirmed, I continued
deeper into the Death Zone, then bore north by northeast for the
Angel, Islington. I knew that one! It was a cheapie on the Monopoly
board game. From Islington it was a short traverse along Holloway
Road for the Sobell.

After spending the evening clawing my way along a brick-lined
corridor fixed with limestone knobs and chalk dust, I had to admit
my inaugural expedition had been a triumphant success. The prin-
ciples of thorough research and planning, adequate provisions and
meticulous navigation had been proven and were all to stand me
in good stead in years to come.

Before long my SS50 and I began making trips deep into the
Weald of Sussex, where I'd mess about on the dank excuse of an
outcrop called Harrison's Rocks. In a matter of weeks, I was ready
to undertake my first full-scale, multi-day international overland
expedition. Destination: the Snowdonia massif in North Wales,
250 miles from Norbury.

The previous December, while the nation had been traumatised by the Sex Pistols' sweary tirade on early-evening TV, I'd discovered the peaks of Snowdonia. The overnight train had arrived in Bangor early in the morning, but there was no prospect of putting up in a hotel or getting a taxi onwards—such decadence was clearly only for spoiled film stars. Instead, I walked the eleven miles to Llanberis, dozing in a bus shelter on the way. That afternoon, I ran out of daylight trying to get to the summit of Snowdon itself. When darkness fell, I ended up digging a snow hole below Snowdon's summit, alongside the mountain lake of Glaslyn. Under the twinkling starlight I dared myself to walk onto the middle of the frozen tarn. I returned with a good idea of where I wanted to spend my spare time in future.

Now that I was independently mobile, there would be no need to walk half the night to a bus shelter. I could simply ride to North Wales like those two hippies in *Easy Rider* and, if I was quick, get in some more snowy-mountain action before the thaw. I scanned the *Reader's Digest Atlas of Great Britain* my dad had bought me as a kid and saw that one road, the A5, led magically all the way from central London to the heart of Snowdonia. All I had to do was memorise the letter A and the number 5.

Originally built by the Romans and once known as Watling Street, the A5 ends at Holyhead on the Welsh island of Anglesey. In the 1800s, it had been the main coaching road linking London with Ireland. For me, too, the A5 has a historical significance: it evokes the overland adventure of getting to North Wales, being there, and getting back. As I was to find in the Sahara years later, accomplishing those three things without incident takes some practice.

The A5 starts in London at Hyde Park. With over 190 miles to cover to the Welsh border post, I had to get a move on. In a haze of naive confidence, I bored resolutely into the dreary late-winter counties north of London at the speed of a trotting Roman legion. Every two minutes, a mile clicked on the odometer of my SS50, the weather held off, and the passing traffic tolerated my presence. But as I neared Nuneaton the engine began to falter; then it picked up, only to die again. I stopped for some petrol. Perhaps the engine needed more "fuel weight" pressing down on it. It made a slight difference but even so, with the afternoon drawing in and barely halfway to the Welsh frontier, I pulled off the A5 to look for lodgings.

Like most people, I'd never heard of Coalville, nor have I come across any reference to it since. But that's where the day ended, in a place with a name like an outback mining town. With the bike playing up, carrying on deeper into the unknown was unwise. I accepted that for the first—but certainly not the last—time, I'd bitten off more than I could chew, and decided to tactically retreat next morning.

When that time came, it wasn't made easy. The snows of Snowdonia had taken pity on me and reached out to carpet the lanes and roofs of Leicestershire. Feet stuck out like outriggers, I slithered back towards the A5, retraced my route along Watling

Street to London, and was home for tea. To paraphrase the guy out of *Jaws*, I was going to need a bigger bike.

Chris Scott is best known for writing the Adventure Motorcycling Handbook, *in print for nearly 30 years, as well as other deserty and overland travel titles. He greatly enjoyed sabotaging that hard-earned profile with* The Street Riding Years *(2016), the recollections of a badly behaved motorcycle messenger in eighties London.*

🌐 *Adventure-Motorcycling.com*
🐦 *@ChrisScottAdv*

STUCK BETWEEN TWO COUNTRIES

By Dylan Wickrama

The following is an excerpt from the book When
the Road Ends. *Used with permission.*

Crossing a border is always special. Crossings give me butterflies
in my stomach. Behind each border post awaits a new language, a
new culture, and so many new things to be discovered and under-
stood. The food smells different and so do the banknotes. The
petrol is more expensive, or cheaper, and the political mood may
be completely different. One's senses have to become accustomed
to whatever is waiting beyond the border. From Cambodia to
Thailand, from Thailand to Laos, the traffic changed sides. From
Sudan to South Sudan, the roads deteriorated immediately after
the border crossing. In South Sudan, there were only six miles of
paved roads in the entire country, the rest is an accumulation of
holes, stones and mud filled irrigation canals.

At other border posts, I had to wait hours at counters, before
being told to queue at another counter for more stamps and documents. It felt like being stuck inside a Kafka novel. And then there
was that border crossing between Egypt and Sudan ...

The border from Egypt to Sudan can only be crossed by ferry.
The two countries are in conflict so the only open border stretches

over Lake Nasser. There is something a little unique about Lake Nasser; the reservoir looks like a Fata Morgana in the dry desert and the landscape along the shore looks like the dry skin of an elephant, caked with mud.

The Nile, the longest river in the world, was staunched for the first time in 1902 at Aswan. The water was regulated in order to prevent flooding and irrigate the land. The original dam was raised twice over the next 32 years and was considered to be the highest construction of its kind. However, the rapidly increasing population of Egypt meant that the dam soon did not hold enough water for dry spells. Therefore, Aswan Dam was built in the Sixties, an enormous structure over 12,500 feet long and 364 feet high. Behind the dam, the water of the Nile accumulated and became Lake Nasser. It reaches across the border more than 200 miles in length and on the Sudanese side the lake's name changes to Lake Nubia.

In October 2010, I reached Aswan on a Monday morning and learnt that the ferry to Wadi Halfa in Sudan sails just once a week, on Monday afternoons. I rushed to the Sudanese consulate in Aswan to get a visa. Even on a trip around the world, Monday mornings can still turn out to be stressful! Upon filling out the application form and handing it in to the consular staff I could do nothing but wait. The minutes passed excruciatingly slowly and turned into hours, until finally, by the time I received the visa, the ferry had long gone.

At least now I had a week to prepare for the crossing. I bought a ticket for the next ferry and started exploring the area by visiting many archaeological sites around Aswan, including the temple complex of Abu Simbel. It had been built between 1290 and 1224 BC during the reign of Rameses II, when the stones were quarried from a single piece of rock. The entire complex was relocated in 1968 to keep it from sinking into the lake. At a cost of 40 million dollars, UNESCO shifted it, cutting it into pieces and rebuilding it 65 yards higher up on the banks of Lake Nasser. Looking up at the massive temple complex, it seems unbelievable that it has not always been where it is now.

The following Monday I made my way to the ferry port, which lies on the eastern side of the mighty dam. The route to Wadi Halfa would take between 18 and 24 hours. Here Bruce (my motorcycle) and I were separated for the crossing. Along with all the other vehicles and crates, Bruce was loaded onto a barge. I, together with a crush of other passengers, crossed the unsteady wooden planks to board the ferry. Before and behind me were men in long white robes; veiled women clutched their children's hands so that they would not be lost in the river of people. More men were pushing and bumping and shoving each other. I became part of this massive surge forward, which eventually ended with us spilling all over the ferry. I was carried along amongst a sea of hands and sweat, unable to control the direction in which I was going.

The barge looked terribly overloaded and the ferry was much the same. Every inch was occupied by passengers and their luggage, and everywhere crates and bags were piled high; some passengers had even made themselves comfortable in the lifeboats. It was hard to find a place to sit, so I squeezed myself into a little space between some crates on the upper deck and tried to find the best position that was least painful. Only those who had booked a private cabin were lucky enough to have a license to stretch.

Travellers with their own vehicles were required to attend the offices of the customs authorities at 9 am on the morning of departure. There were fifteen of us, ten bikers who were in a hurry, travelling from the north of Finland to South Africa in 25 days; a Swedish couple, about as old as their VW bus, on their way to Ethiopia; a Belgian father and son travelling in a Land Rover down to the Cape of Good Hope; and me. We all had to comply with the formalities which involved a lot of red tape. We had to fill in about fifty different forms and it had to be done in Arabic. We then had to get them stamped by fifty different clerks, in the right order, and only then could we return the local license plates which every vehicle had received upon entry into the country. Then, finally, we could obtain a certificate from a judge stating that we had not been in conflict with the law during our stay in Egypt.

We tourists were treated as a group and all had to wait until the last one of us had completed our formalities. Five hours later, we were escorted down to the harbour by policemen and the vehicles were loaded onto the barge, one by one. The long waiting and the endless formalities made us bond. After five hours at the customs office, you stop being strangers. We passed the time telling stories from our travels and on the ferry we continued to get to know one another even better.

The only other way of passing the time, besides chatting to fellow passengers, was to take a little walk to the other end of the ferry to stretch your legs. This quickly turned into a steeplechase.

The majority of the passengers that used the ferry were traders of Sudanese origin. They had flown from Khartoum to Aswan to buy trading items in bulk and then travelled by ferry back to Sudan, as it was cheaper than by air. Hardly had the ferry left the harbour when all the merchants began to unpack their goods and repack them shrewdly. Two packs of light bulbs became one. Three packets of spices were stuffed into a single packet and so on and so forth. The merchants were old hands at decreasing the numbers of their goods, thus reducing the import duties. Although there were customs officers on board the ferry, nobody seemed bothered about it.

The volume of noise climbed as high as the soaring thermometer. The roaring ship engines continued their never-ending bassline as a contrast to the stillness of the desert. In fact I wished I was somewhere far away out there in the sands, so that I could enjoy the desert silence. But since I knew that this was just a one-time hassle, I gladly endured it.

Shortly before sunset, the Sudanese immigration officers began collecting everyone's passports. All formalities had to be completed before our arrival in Wadi Halfa. I reached into my shirt pocket. Empty! I opened the bag where I had stored all my documents in a folder. Everything was there except the passport! Then I searched the backpack. Nothing! The last place to check was the camera bag, but my passport was not there either. Frantically I racked my brain ... where had I left the stupid thing? And then it dawned on me. It was safely tucked away in one of Bruce's panniers and Bruce, my BMW GS1150, was travelling on the barge and was already out of sight, as the barge was much slower.

The officials were none too pleased about my missing passport and told me that I would be unable to disembark without it. I would have to wait until the barge reached Wadi Halfa. Not a problem, I thought, I need to wait for Bruce either way. A few passengers who were familiar with the route told me that the ferry remained in the harbour in Wadi Halfa for one whole day before returning to Egypt. "By then, the cargo ship will have reached the harbour. Don't worry!" I was reassured, but still spent the night sleeping uncomfortably among the crates and luggage, turning and twisting every thirty seconds.

When we reached the harbour of Wadi Halfa the next day, the sun was at its highest point.

The word "harbour" is perhaps a little exaggerated to describe the dock and the few bollards that were used to moor the ferry, with the vast Sudanese desert landscape stretching out behind it and without any hint of civilization. I watched as the noisy crowd disembarked. Some were welcomed by relatives; others haggled with a taxi driver to take them into town. Whilst my friends tried to explain my situation to the officials to get me off the ferry, the rest of the passengers took off in taxis and overcrowded mini-buses. Emptied of people, the dock became quiet and my 14 friends called out to me from the pier that I had to remain on the ferry for now. I thanked them and yelled that I would "See you tomorrow!" when they returned to collect their vehicles. They clambered into the last minibus and drove off.

Without the passengers on the ferry, it suddenly felt much larger. For want of anything better to do, I stared at the horizon for hours, hoping to see the cargo barge carrying Bruce. Finally, the crew invited me to share a meal with them. They even gave me a private cabin where I could sleep and shower.

When I stepped on deck the next day, I was refreshed. I scoured the lake for the barge, but there was no sign of it. I scanned the horizon—nothing. There were still five hours left before the ferry was due to depart. I was certain the barge would arrive at any moment. After breakfast, I resumed my position at the railing and kept watch until my eyes began to water. Nothing happened. The lake was quiet and there was no sign of anything, and the crew informed me that they had no means to communicate with the cargo vessel. Even though the officials had been very clear that they would not let me leave the ship without a passport, I tried my luck once more when they came back aboard to accompany the next batch of passengers across the border. As soon as they saw me, they put on grim faces. They felt no pity for me. If they had hearts, then they were hiding them behind their faded, light blue uniforms very effectively. The crew got involved, tried to appease the officials and cheer me up. Apparently, nobody could remember the ferry leaving for Egypt before the barge had arrived in Wadi

Halfa. Surely everything would work itself out. If necessary, they would be able to delay the departure of the ferry a little ... or at least I kept telling myself that.

The planned time of departure came and went and still there was no sign of the barge. Still more luggage continued to be loaded and more passengers embarked. My optimism was replaced by an increasing nervousness. After two more hours, the cargo vessel had still not shown up. This time there were fewer passengers— this crossing would be more comfortable than the last—but I really couldn't bear the thought of going back to Aswan! I did not feel like spending another week in that place and crossing that damn lake two more times! And besides, what would happen to Bruce in this godforsaken place if he was not collected for a week?

As the hours of uneventful waiting passed, my edginess increased accordingly.

I had to take action!

I would simply stay here! If necessary, I would jump off the ferry and swim ashore. The ferry was only about fifteen feet high—no problem. I was fed up with this ferry and angry at the obstinate officials but mostly just annoyed with myself for forgetting the passport.

My situation soon became known among the few passengers who were travelling to Aswan that day. While we were waiting in the harbour, I chatted to an Englishman and a Sudanese gentleman. I asked them if they would throw my luggage onto the pier if I jumped off the ferry just as it was leaving, without the knowledge of the crew. My idea was to jump into the water sneakily and then swim ashore, so that by the time the officials discovered me, the ferry would already be gone. The Englishman and the Sudanese man looked at each other, and then both lifted their eyebrows and began to counsel me as if we were standing on the Golden Gate Bridge and I was about to put an end to it all. But once I convinced them that it wasn't an attempted suicide, they agreed to help me out.

When the ferry was about four hours behind schedule, the captain could wait no longer. He started the engine, the ropes were taken off the bollards, and the ferry began to move. Dirty brown water churned beneath us, until it was pulled into the maelstrom of the ship's propeller. Looking down into the tumultuous waters, I contemplated my plan, but the ugly broth, combined with the words of the Sudanese and the Englishman who had pointed out that such a stunt could create the opportunity for the officials to refuse my entry even with a passport, convinced me that my plan was futile. I resigned myself to my fate.

We had not been moving for five minutes when in the horizon the outline of a dark object appeared. I could have screamed! Just five minutes earlier I had longed for this to happen, but now I was cursing. Why had that stupid thing not shown up a little sooner!

I ran up to the captain, who by now I knew personally, and tried to convince him to go as closely as possible to the barge so that I would be able to jump over. A crew member translated my words into Arabic. The captain, who looked more like Allah's messenger in his long white robe, discussed this with his men. They hesitated, and did not seem too keen on my plan.

In my urgency, their discussion seemed to take forever. In truth, it can't have been more than a minute before the guy who spoke English announced the result, "Yes, the captain will try, but it is difficult. We have not done this before."

Their words did not sound as confident as I would have liked them to be.

Another hour passed until we came closer to the barge with its—for me, at least—precious cargo: Bruce and my passport. But the ferry captain was not trying hard enough to get close to the barge. In fact, it passed us by a mile and I could just about see Bruce through the zoom lens of my camera. Even I had to admit that nobody would be able to swim that far in a crocodile-infested lake. The Sudanese man and the Englishman were noticeably relieved when they saw that I had given up my plan. But my eyes followed the barge for as long as I could see it.

We continued through the hot desert landscape. The stifling air was cooled by the water, making it bearable, but it was still hot enough to feel uncomfortable. I was glad that the ferry was half empty. Everyone found a little spot in the shade where they could stretch their legs and doze. In the dead of the night, we passed by the illuminated temple complex of Abu Simbel. While the other passengers marvelled at its beauty, it held no charm for me. I had seen the temple three times already and would go past it again for a fourth time soon.

The accent of another passenger revealed that she came from Switzerland, like me. Her name was Karin and she had worked as a project volunteer for a year in Tanzania, but was now homeward bound. She had already heard about my situation and said that she might be able to help. Whilst waiting for the ferry in Wadi Halfa, she had made friends with the family of the customs clearing agent. Karin reached for her mobile and called the agent. She didn't waste any time, got straight to the point and told the man at the other end that he would have to take care of my motorcycle and that under no circumstances was it to be sent back, as this would mean—and I shuddered when I imagined it—that Bruce and I would cross each other's paths again next week. She also told the agent that the motorcycle would need to be covered by a plastic sheet, so that the desert dust would not damage it. I shook my head. Bruce would cope just fine. He is an adventurer just like me and to coddle him like that was almost an insult, but Karin was adamant. The agent promised to keep Bruce and to keep him safely covered until my return to Wadi Halfa.

A few hours later, the Egyptian border guards began to collect the passports. That game again! "Without a passport, you cannot go ashore," they told me.

"Till next week? Until we go back?"

"That's right. If your passport is in Wadi Halfa, you will have to remain on board."

This possibility had not even occurred to me until now. I had to restrain myself from getting into an argument and making the officers angry. The ferry did not seem to want to let me go.

The young Swiss woman came to my rescue for a second time. A year in Africa had apparently taught her how to deal with obstinate officials. Without missing a beat, she said to me, "Just wait, we'll get you out of the tight corner."

I watched in fascination as she began a charm offensive which would have been irresistible for even the Pope to withstand. Karin was pretty and she knew it. She paid the officers compliments; she laughed at their silly jokes, played with her blonde hair, and smiled at one and then winked at the next. She asked questions, showed interest, and it even seemed to me that her neckline sat a little bit lower than before.

Karin's flirting seemed to be working. Once she had charmed the men sufficiently, she brought my miserable situation to their attention.

"How unkind it would be to make him stay on the boat for a whole week," she said with a pitiful face.

Suddenly, the uniformed men were much friendlier than before.

After some vacillation and deliberation, they concluded that I would be able to leave the ferry with a special permit. But only on one condition: I had to pay 15 dollars for a new visa. Fifteen dollars for my freedom for a week? I would have gladly paid them double! They gave me a small piece of cardboard onto which they glued my picture. It was stamped and my name was handwritten onto it in Arabic, phonetically. Karin beamed, "What did I tell you?"

It goes without saying that her dinner was on me that night.

Monday soon came round and I went to the ferry port—again. The director of the Aswan ferry even gave me a free ticket and food vouchers for the next crossing. They had told me that I was the first person ever to be refused permission to leave the ferry in Wadi Halfa and sent back to Aswan, and that everybody on the Egyptian side was apologetic for what I had to endure at the hands of the harsh Sudanese.

Back on the ferry, there was the same hustle and bustle as the week before. Apart from the passengers, everybody knew me by my name and I was almost part of the crew. The pungent smells, the noise, and the stuffiness of the quay embraced me, the oily ferry engines greeted me and from the galley, the smell of boiled beans wafted up as I prepared myself for the crossing, much more relaxed than the last time. Two Germans who I had met at the hostel in Aswan offered me the floor in their private cabin to spend the night. It was rather cramped, but better than sharing the deck with hundreds of other passengers.

At night, the passports were collected. Ha! I already knew this game, but I still couldn't play along. The Sudanese duty officials were as unfriendly as ever and they clearly did not like me much. My passport was waiting for me at the port, I explained as amiably as possible, something which they already knew. But they were unimpressed. They repeated the same message as before—they would not let me get off the ferry in Wadi Halfa without a passport. Somebody was clearly enjoying their power. I smiled, told them in German what I thought of them and decided to let them play their game.

Many hours later, the engines quietened down, indicating that we had reached Wadi Halfa. I was tense, but the clearing agent stood at the quay, as punctual as a Swiss watch. As soon as we got close enough, I threw him the motorbike keys and told him where to find my passport. He ran towards Bruce who was indeed hidden beneath a plastic sheet and returned a few minutes later, waving the red passport in the midday heat. What a relief!

Before the officials could devise further difficulties, the agent was on board and I was once again the proud owner of a passport. The officials grudgingly stamped it and Bruce and I resumed our journey.

More than two years after that adventure, I was in Vancouver and faced with similar problems. It was just as stupid to lose Bruce's original documents as it had been to not have one's own passport. While I waited for my brother to send me a new vehicle registration from Switzerland, I heard that Bruce had arrived. Even though all I had was just a printed email, I tried my luck and found that Canadian officials are much more easy-going. Just a single form later, and without having to show any documentation, I collected Bruce from the customs warehouse. I was relieved and pleasantly surprised, but also a little concerned; could someone else, anyone else, have collected Bruce? But nothing else mattered. At last I was reunited with my companion.

If you travel with a motorcycle for such a long time and in the same manner as I did, it becomes your best friend, your home, and your conversation partner. No wonder I was looking forward so much to seeing him again—and he was just as excited to see me.

Wickrama means "adventure," and one doesn't need any further words to describe the character of this man. Growing up in Sri Lanka shaped the way Dylan lives and travels today: always open for a bigger challenge.

In 2010, Dylan sold his automobile repair shop, which he had built up over six years in Switzerland, and invested the money wisely in traveling around the world with a motorcycle which he affectionately calls Bruce—a 2004 model BMW GS1150 ADV. Three years after setting off, he arrived in Panama, where all roads suddenly end because of the infamous "Darién." Undefeated by this new situation, Dylan decided to build a raft out of ten oil drums—powered by Bruce the motorcycle—and set sail on the Pacific Ocean in search of Colombia.

Dylan published his book When the Road Ends in 2015. Today he continues to live life mainly on the road through many inspirational talks he holds internationally. He also leads guided motorcycle tours and works as a freelance photographer and author.

🌐 Ride2xplore.com
📷 @ride2xplore
📘 /ride2xplore

FINDING PEACE

By Liz Jansen

Wilderness parted before me as I rode north to Peace River Country, 500 kilometres north of Edmonton, Alberta. Frontier country. Wild. Beautiful. Unpredictable. The highway followed a broad valley and the courageous river that had carved its way through the boreal forest eons ago. Between the road and the river ran a steel ribbon, defying the elements. River, rail, and road. Fingers that reached out, transporting explorers, settlers, and prospectors to their dreams. In 1926, the rail had carried my paternal grandfather, 26-year-old Johann Klassen, my grandmother Elizabeth (Liese) Friesen, and their infant Bennie, who would become my father, north to a new life near Beaverlodge. I was going up to meet my grandfather for the first time.

My Triumph Tiger and I were 4,000 kilometres from home, on a quest that had begun more than two years earlier. That attempt came to an abrupt end three weeks after it started when I crashed in southern Alberta. I'd totalled my motorcycle, sustained a complex shoulder fracture, and embarked on an unplanned time of healing. Now we'd resumed that journey, following what I'd dubbed the Ancestor Trail, tracing the migration of my grandparents after they'd landed in Canada as refugees in the 1920s. I wanted to walk the land they'd walked, feel its energy, and imagine myself in their place as best I could. What had life been like? How had it inured them? How did their experiences live in me?

All my grandparents were German-speaking Russian Mennonites. Impoverished in body but not spirit, they were part of an exodus of 20,000 Mennonites from an area of what is now Ukraine, where their ancestors had prospered for more than 100 years. Their farms were fertile and verdant, visited by Russian government leaders and esteemed as models for other colonies. For many of them, life had been very good. Until it wasn't.

The Russian revolution in 1917 ushered in a reign of terror and gruesome atrocities, particularly against German-speaking citizens. Five years of civil war, compounded by drought, famine, and hyperinflation, almost wiped them out.

Love finds a way even in chaos and so, in 1920, Johann and Liese married. Two daughters arrived within the next four years. Although it looked like some semblance of order might return to the country, Johann foresaw trouble and made preparations to bring his family to a land where they could live in peace and freedom. Another scourge, typhus, would take both daughters a month before they were to leave. It would only be two of them, and the new life that grew in Liese.

After making it out of Russia by boxcar, they'd been delayed in England while Johann was treated for trachoma (an eye infection). Their arrival in Canada had been three months later than planned, but others in their group had gone before and would be waiting. Heading into a remote wilderness in the middle of winter, not sure what awaited them or where they'd live, was not ideal, for Liese was about to give birth. Instead, they waited in Swalwell, Alberta until Bennie was born two months later before completing their journey.

What had been going through Johann's mind as he looked out the train window, through mile after mile of mixed coniferous forests laced with wetlands and lakes? The landscape around Swalwell had reassured him because it reminded him of the steppe he'd farmed with his father, and his father before him. Had he made the right decision for his family? He'd lived in a big brick farmhouse in a small village, but the communities were all networked. Family lived at his fingertips. Now he and Liese would be with fewer than twenty families, spread out across the countryside. But a name like Peace River had to be a good sign.

He must have been relieved to see the land finally transition from forest to field. He could picture their farm and home here. It would be hard at first, but nothing compared to what they'd come through. And it would be a good life for his family.

Beaverlodge was known as Redlow at that time, but my family always referred to the area as Peace River, no doubt in unconscious reference to finally finding a land of peace. When Johann arrived, a year after the railroad extension's completion, less than 200 people lived here, clustered around a post office, school, and a few stores. It became Beaverlodge in 1929, named after the lodges built along the river by the Beaver Indians.

The population has grown to 2,465 but retains that pioneer edge. As I rode alongside the railway tracks on the main route through town, massive, mud-covered four-wheel-drive pickup trucks dwarfed me. The pavement even had a film of slick mud on this sunny August day, vestiges of forays into surrounding fields.

A more convivial aspect of frontier towns is their welcome to strangers, especially women on motorcycles travelling alone. In most northern municipalities, somewhere in town is a spartan and well-maintained campground. I found the Beaverlodge Pioneer Campground right beside the IGA grocery store, tucked in behind a former one-room log schoolhouse. This would be home for the next three days while I explored the area.

Travellers have been stopping by for more than a hundred years, although their characteristics have changed. At one time, prospectors came here on their way to gold fields and their dreams of fortune. In the late 1920s when Johann arrived, settlers poured out of rail cars to homestead land on the traditional territories of the people of the Treaty 8 region. Now the campsite sees more pickups hauling fifth wheels, filled with families and vacationing retired people. There were even three young men from New Brunswick who'd come to work in the oil fields. And one motorcyclist in a tent. I had a shaded, grassy plot, solid picnic tables, clean showers, electricity, and free Wi-Fi from the secondary school behind me. It was perfect.

It's easy to understand why this land appealed to farmers. Prairie grasslands roll up from the south in gentle undulations, creating a sense of openness. Foothills of the Rockies flank the western exposure and abundant forests protect the northern and eastern edges. A small stream squiggles its way through, as if trying to have as much fun as possible before joining the modest Beaverlodge River. Back in Johann's day, the land would have been rife with deer, elk, moose, black bear, small mammals, waterfowl, and songbirds; the rivers would have teemed with fish. Even now, in August, the area felt lush, and dense crops covered fields maturing for harvest.

I intended to find the exact location of the farm from instructions that were approximate—near the cemetery where Johann lay. Sketchy directions told me to turn south at Foster's Feed and Seed, continue over the bridge, and look for a grove of trees with a sign to mark the cemetery.

I meandered south, crossing the concrete bridge, taking in the surroundings, and not wanting to miss what I knew was an overgrown plot. I needn't have worried. The sign on the east side of the road was much larger than I expected, worn and tired, but standing tall against a backdrop of tall poplars. The gravel shoulder was too narrow and sloped to park on. Since few vehicles travelled the road, I crowded the edge of the pavement, kicked out the side stand, and turned on the four-way flashers. Dismounting, I removed my helmet as one would doff a hat out of respect, then walked across the road, reading across the deep ditch, a chasm of time.

Beaverlodge River Mennonite Cemetery

The Mennonite families purchased land in this area in the late 1920s, establishing their cemetery on their site, and further north, their church. It served them until roads and transportation improved, and they centralized near LaGlace. This graveyard, not being registered, was partially destroyed with the building of the present bridge and road.

Rest in Peace.

County of Grande Prairie, 1977

I knew the graves had been disturbed and my grandfather's remains had likely been moved during road renovations, but to stand there taking it in overwhelmed me. This is where he lay. This man's blood runs in my veins and his strength has shaped me. Were it not for his endurance in getting his family here, my story would be very different.

I needed to find out where he'd lived. A small frame house on this side of the bridge had caught my attention so I made a U-turn, stopping at the mailbox. A large mongrel loped up the muddy, rutted driveway, barking and friendly-looking, but I wasn't willing to test him by pulling into a situation I couldn't get out of. As I stopped to consider my next move, a curious woman approached.

She listened as I described my mission, then invited me to join her family gathered in the side yard.

Her grandfather and his brother had purchased large tracts of land around 1914, homesteading and making homesteading arrangements with other settlers. She'd heard stories about the Mennonite families who had landed here and had seen pictures of their log homes and gatherings. But she didn't know how I could find out exactly where my grandparents and infant father had called home.

Land records are archived at the county seat in Grande Prairie, 40 kilometres east, back across a bucolic route, now golden. Mary, the archivist who knew every dusty document in that library, pulled out huge ledger books filled with meticulous entries made by a clerk wielding a fountain pen trailing fine black ink. I pored through them, deciphering the elaborate cursive, but no title bore my grandfather's name. Ironically, the only record of him being in the area was an official entry for what was purported to be an unregistered cemetery. He was the second of eight people interred there, including one other man and six infants.

Disappointed, but not defeated, I returned to Beaverlodge. Knowing my family had lived close to the cemetery, I'd use my intuition to guide me. That would have to do.

Township roads are laid out in a grid. I followed them up, down, and across, pausing at regular intervals to get off my bike, walk around, and take in the view. What had Johann thought as he'd built his log home and barns, and the life for his family? Climate and soil conditions were perfect and the yield high that first summer, like his spirits. He'd survived extreme hardship, left his daughters on Russian soil, and said goodbye to parents and other family, knowing he'd never see them again. But he'd persevered, and now he and his family could enjoy life in freedom. Everything looked so promising.

And then the cough and night sweats started. I'm sure he tried to ignore them for as long as he could. He was young and healthy and could beat this. But tuberculosis was incurable. When there was no other choice, he was moved to Grande Prairie and the log building that served as a hospital, isolated from his family. He must have worried how they'd manage. It had been a hard life for Liese, my grandmother, too, and now he'd be adding to that, leaving her a widow at twenty-seven with a small son. Although he spoke fluent English, she spoke German, and they'd have no one to support them. He'd survived many challenges, but he didn't have the strength to overcome this one. He died on February 7, 1928, less than two years after arriving in this land of peace.

Motorcycles are ideal for processing thoughts, and I had a lot to consider. Peace River Country's expansive terrain is perfect for the job. Besides, I wouldn't likely pass this way again and wanted to explore this land that had drawn so many with dreams of a better life. I'd already been on the road for two weeks and it would have been good to have a day off and ponder everything I'd seen as I'd ridden further north than I'd ever been on my motorcycle.

Heavy fog blanketed the town the next day. A check of the weather station showed it would clear about twenty kilometres away, so I waited a bit for it to dissipate, then set out. Mother Earth has been particularly prolific and giving in Peace River country, sustaining life in a variety of ways. Not only is there harvest from prime farmland, but beneath the surface is a network of pipes drawing oil from her depths. Tanker trucks trundle down gravel roads and traverse farm fields to sidle up to pumping stations. After gorging on liquid gold, they deliver it to larger pumping stations or refineries. Further north, the harvest turns to lumber and logging trucks replace tankers, their racks bulging with freshly felled trees.

Then the land drops away and the road sweeps right as it descends into a dramatic valley. There, at its heart, is the mighty Peace River, flowing as it has for eons. Mighty. Broad. Languid. Powerful.

There's no designated place to stop, but I had to. With little traffic and good visibility, I hit the kill switch and balanced on the side of the road to take in the view, the air, and the energy. Nothing can match the sheer beauty or power of nature.

I could have stayed for hours, but more country awaited. With my motorcycle taking the lead, I continued down and across an enormous bridge before letting the road carry me back around sweeping curves, up and out of the deep valley, back onto flat land. The beauty was so surreal, it felt like I'd dreamt the experience.

There had been very little opportunity to ride along the river but according to the map, I could take a side road before the town of Peace River and do just that. From the turnoff, there was little to suspect the landscape would change, but suddenly, I found myself catching my breath again at the scene that unfolded. It was as if the landscape were protecting a great treasure until the last moment. Powerless to do anything else, I stopped to absorb it. The valley here was straight and offered a glimpse of the town in the distance. Another steep, curving descent flattened out on the valley floor, leading me to the river's edge and the road that hugged its contours. It wasn't long enough. After following it for several kilometres and crossing another gigantic bridge, I arrived in the town of Peace River.

It was already mid-afternoon and I'd gone further and taken longer than expected, but the landscape has a way of drawing in the unsuspecting traveller. After a quick tour of the museum and a late lunch on its grounds overlooking the river, it was time to head back on a different route. By the time I reached my campsite, I'd covered 611 glorious kilometres.

With one day left, I wanted to savour the area and pay final respects to my ancestors. Nearing the cemetery again, I noted a culvert for farm access. It gave me a safe spot to park as well as access to the site without having to climb through the ditch.

This time I followed farm truck tracks to behind the copse, the roadside cemetery sign occluded by trees. The drone from stacks of beehives provided background music as I took in the tangle of greenery. None of the graves was marked or even visible, and there was no evidence to even suggest anyone had ever been there. I wondered about the experiences of the people who had tried to tame this land. The people whose dreams had set the stage for future generations.

But I was only interested in one person. After all the courage and hardship he'd been through, getting to this land, getting his family here, and then leaving them to fend for themselves, I wondered, how did he feel as he prepared to enter the afterlife. Had he had a calm or troubled passing?

Softly, I called to him. "Opa, are you here?"

From nowhere, a bird appeared high above my head, soaring towards the trees in front of me before swooping away, back to where it came from. A messenger.

"No, little one, not in the trees, but I'm here with you and in the wind. I'm at peace."

Johann had found what he'd sought for himself and his family.

"Thank you, Opa. We are well. Rest in peace."

Four months after my visit, aided by the Alberta Genealogical Society, I received the probate file for Johann's estate. It specified the exact location of six quarter-sections he and three other families farmed in an arrangement with the ancestors of the woman I spoke with. My intuition had guided me there. Although I didn't know exactly where their log house had stood, I'd been on their land, including the cemetery placed on a corner of one of those quarter-sections.

Liz Jansen began riding a motorcycle on her family farm when she was sixteen. She could not have imagined how transformative her two-wheeled experiences would be, or how powerful a teacher and muse motorcycling was. In 2003, she left a career in corporate human resources and training and development and built a business around demonstrating that when you've mastered two wheels, you can master anything.

Her desire to understand personal perspectives and life choices led her to study Shamanic Energy Medicine. She's learned that how life unfolds is determined by the stories we tell ourselves, the stories we've embraced, and the stories that have been passed down for generations—stories we're often not aware we're carrying. Through her writing, speaking, and Energy Medicine practice, she helps others see how we can change our life by changing those stories.

Liz is the author of Women, Motorcycles and the Road to Empowerment, *and* Life Lessons from Motorcycles. *Her latest book,* Crash Landing, The Long Way Home, *explores how the experiences of our ancestors shape us. Or, who we are before we're told who we are. She lives in Orangeville, Ontario, Canada.*

FIRING ON ALL CYLINDERS

By Sam Manicom

The Outback of Australia is my kind of country, with my kind of climate. I feel more alive when it's hot. Part of me seems to go into mental hibernation in the cold, but when it's warm I fire on all cylinders, most of the time.

Australia was the perfect place to head to after my year-long ride the length of Africa. I'd been due to return home to the UK from southern Africa, but the more I'd thought about it, there simply hadn't been a good enough reason to do that. Overlanding was a buzz. I was hungry for more. I'd booked passage for myself and my BMW R80GS on a container ship from Durban to Sydney, and the new adventure was already rolling.

The Great Dividing Range, which splits the east coast of Australia from the Outback, comes really close to the coast in Queensland. It acts as a craggy line between the populated and much-visited coastal areas, and the mostly barren inland regions. The Outback gets little of the coastal rains, but when it does, the dry scrublands briefly come alive with vibrant greens and the startling colours of flowers.

I dropped out of the range along the Flinders Highway into a land of dusty sidetracks, one-horse towns, and vegetation that never really seemed to change. I should have been cruising through a giant garden, but this year the rains were late, so no such luck. The scrubby trees, where there were any, were all the same height. Sometimes these sporadic trees would suddenly become the temporary resting places for flocks of brightly coloured parakeets or galahs. The flocks of cockatoos were my favorites, though.

These birds, who seemed to be either black or white, were all comedians. Sometimes I saw them settle on electric or telephone wires, and when they did so it was rather like watching a bunch of circus clowns attempting to walk the high wire. They'd fall off, wings fluttering madly to great shrieks of pretend dismay until they had almost reached the ground, when they would miraculously recover and shoot up for another session of Charlie Chaplin-style walking the line. The equally scrubby, spindly bushes all seemed to be the same height, too, and shade was at a premium. Their thin leaves didn't offer much protection at all, and the soil only changed in shade of red where a slight amount of moisture remained in the early hours. I saw small birds sitting on the power lines, but only where they could sit in the shade of the isolators. The road ran straight and the asphalt collected heat from a sun that hung in a cloudless sky. This sky is amazing. It's an everlasting transparent electric blue and it hangs above desert lands that seem to have been stunned by the silence.

From time to time, I eased off the highway to do a little scrub riding. It's so deserted in this area that I felt total confidence in off-loading all my kit from the bike, leaving it behind a bush, and then playing on the tracks. They were an adventure, but not only was the exercise good for the body, the mental challenge was good for the grey cells. "Bull dust" just confused them, though. It's a very fine powdery dust that collects on the tracks and to me looked just like ordinary sand, so I never had any warning. A couple of times I hit great pans of the stuff at speed, and instantly felt as if I'd run into the middle of an enormous red blancmange. My wheels would slop around in the deep, slippery dust and the air would be so full of the fine particles that in larger pans I'd almost get disoriented. The dust gave my face a sort of red monster look, and would instantly turn into glue when mixed with sweat. But whatever size the dustpans were, they always got my heart beating a bit faster. Some of that came from the effort of picking the bike up after I'd taken a tumble.

Back on the asphalt, we settled into a cruising speed of about 90 kilometres per hour. Everything seemed totally in sync, my luggage was nicely balanced, my bike seemed to be enjoying the open road, and the tread on my new tyres hummed beneath us. With very few bends, the road seemed to disappear over the horizon, with an occasional pothole and truck tyre "tramlines" providing just about the only element of adventure. Monster trucks drive helter-skelter along these roads, and their sheer weight is enough to form gullies in the heat-softened asphalt. The grit-covered tar was so hot in the middle of the day that my feet felt like they were cooking in my bike boots.

When the midday heat grew, I flipped my visor closed. Riding these temperatures was like sitting in front of an enormous hair dryer at max temperature setting, going full blast. The asphalt-stored heat hammered up at me in shimmering waves, and mirages jigged deceptive dances on the road. I was sweating like I hadn't since I'd ridden through Northern Africa. My mouth struggled to keep moist, so drink breaks were vital, but the water in my new bottles was decidedly unappetizing—it was almost hot enough to make tea. A tip I'd picked up when getting ready to ride Africa was the solution. My water bottles were in canvas bags, strapped over the petrol tank. I carefully punched a hole in the tops of two of the bottles, and as I rode a little water escaped onto the canvas of the bags. That moisture would then whip away in my slipstream and this form of sweating meant that the water in the bottles was almost cool; a delight after my attempts to drink hot swimming pool.

Even so, the dream of an ice-cold Coke stayed with me across the gently undulating bushland for so long that I just had to have one. It became an obsession. The trouble was, there were no shops and pubs were few and far between. Getting enough to drink was always an issue.

So were bush fires. The land is as dry as a tinderbox and it doesn't take much to start a bush fire. It could be a carelessly discarded cigarette, a match dropped out of the window of a passing vehicle, or simply a piece of broken glass. The results are horrific. I'd ridden past hundreds of kilometres of bushland that had been stripped of all colours except black. The world was a soft, sooty black carpet that was only broken by the stark shape of occasional trees whose twisted limbs had been big enough to remain standing, lonely silhouettes in a plain of devastation. I'd survived a bush fire in Africa and had no wish for a repeat performance.

Challenges also came from the tramline-making road trains. These beasts are kings of the road and their drivers blast their way up the highway at such speed you'd think that the next pub had the last beers left in Australia. Their trailers swing from side to side, and their pure bulk makes a sucking slipstream. It's enough to make eyeballs pop and knuckles go white in the attempt to stay upright and away from those hurtling wheels. There are so many, that if you did get sucked in, you'd be mincemeat in seconds and the truck driver would never even notice. I decided that discretion was the better part of valour and I pulled over whenever I saw a road train coming. The long, open road meant I could see the trains coming from kilometres away, but regular use of my mirrors was vital—often the trucks would be going faster than I wanted to. They had a living to earn. I was just travelling.

The next pub was a trucker's stop. Weathered board with peeling paint clad the walls; the roof was tin, and the parking area was a great spread of oily dirt that had still managed to keep a few ruts that must have been made with the last rains. Everything was dust-covered, tired, and shimmering with listless heat. Three four-trailer road-train trucks were parked alongside a couple of beaten-up Toyota Land Cruiser pickup trucks—"utes" as they are usually known (short for utility trucks). Next to them was a battered Land

Rover of 1960s vintage, and a white Holden estate car that had, in the dim and distant past, probably been someone's pride and joy. Each vehicle had a giant set of tubular bars attached to its front, and one of the pickup truck's bars was decidedly bent. A sheep dog lay in the shade of the veranda, but even with my unusual arrival, it made no effort to do anything other than twitch an ear. I parked in the shade of one of the trucks, and immediately took my jacket off—then my helmet. The jacket came off first, because if it didn't I'd instantly feel like I was boiling over.

There were three bars: saloon, lounge, and ladies' bar. I was chuffed to see the last one, as I knew that they were an important part of Outback history. In days gone by, it was considered improper for women to drink in the same bar as men, and with the language that was in full flow in the saloon bar, I could see why. Ladies' bars are supposed to be a thing of the past, though. I stepped into the saloon, and let my eyes get used to the gloom and my body used to the surprising cool. As I did so, all conversation stopped dead, and all eyes turned towards me, but the loud chat quickly resumed as I moved across the bare wooden boards towards the bar.

The sight of a skinny Pommie in dusty bike gear ordering a Coke in this environment was sufficient for everyone to lose any interest in me at all. That was fine, as it gave me a chance to discreetly watch the men in the room. In front of each was an amber-coloured beer; the glasses were small, with dew on the sides where hot fingers hadn't recently touched them. All the men were clad in stained shorts and singlets or T-shirts. Boots that probably hadn't seen any polish since they'd been new were the norm and yes, there were more than a few wide-brimmed, sweat-stained hats on heads. Conversation was pure bloke—trucks, women, beer, the next load, a bastard copper, the footie, and farming. It seemed that for every five words, there'd be a swear word thrown in for good measure, in case the listeners hadn't got the point. Suddenly, all conversation stopped again.

Into the bar had stepped an academic-looking, youngish man who, heaven forbid, was accompanied by a very pretty girl. Like me, they had "tourist" stamped all over them. All the men turned round in their seats and stared in silence so intensely that the two caught the message, and rapidly retreated. Not a word had been spoken—looks had done it. I was sitting in a room full of dinosaurs, who didn't seem to realise that they ought soon to be extinct.

My two iced Cokes had gone too quickly and, with water bottles filled, I stepped out into the heat again. At two o'clock in the afternoon, it was almost a wall of heat out there, and even the dog's ear didn't twitch this time.

Riding in the cool of South Australia and along the coast had made me lazy, and I knew that it was time for me to change my riding habits. It made a lot of sense to set off in the cool of the dawn and ride only until midday. Or find somewhere to hole up in the shade during the main heat of the day, then ride on in the cooling hours until dark. The risk out here was that dawn and dusk are the play times for kangaroos, and I'd already seen how much damage they could do to a pickup—they would be lethal to me on the bike.

I'd not seen any live kangaroos at all, but there had been plenty of fly-infested, stinking, furry bundles by the roadsides. Some had been no bigger than a large dog, but others had been big enough, I suspected, to have been able to damage even a big truck. There were very few road signs along the way, but those that punctuated the roadsides with their vivid yellow frequently warned of kangaroos. Obliquely, since they were almost always shot up, they also warned of bored drivers with guns.

One of the advantages of long, open roads like this is that there are plenty of places to pull off the highway to wild camp. That was good for my budget, and I loved camping in the middle of nowhere, with only the stars for company.

Falling into the new routine, I set off the next morning in the peach and blueberry shades of dawn. The air was gently warm and though I could still feel the remainder of the previous day's heat coming off the asphalt at me, the riding was good. The 'roos stayed away from me, and I settled into the saddle for another day's cruising on a road with enough dips for me to feel as if I were riding along a gently graded roller coaster. By midmorning the heat was intense again, and I started to look for some shade in which to rest and have a drink. My eyelids began to droop, and a bead of sweat found its way into my left eye. The sting of the salt was enough to wake me up—I'd been dozing at 90 kilometres per hour! I had to stop and have a sleep, but it had to be in shade, so I rode on, searching the scrubby horizon for a stand of trees. Then I woke up again! The bike was heading straight for the bush—another second's sleep and I'd have been flung off, with potentially disastrous consequences. I'd allowed myself to get too sleepy to be awake to the risk I was taking by riding on.

One of my favourite items of my multi-purpose travel kit is my sarong. Not only is it perfect for a stroll to the shower on a camping site, for a dash for the bushes in the dark, or to lie on for a spot of sunbathing, but it also works brilliantly as a sun shade. With no trees in sight, it was up to me to make my own shade. With my sarong strung from the side of my bike I settled down for an hour's kip. I was asleep within seconds.

Whilst coming up the east coast I'd heard all sorts of scare stories about bikers who had been totally unprepared for the Outback—they had either come a cropper or had disappeared, never to be seen again. One chap had obviously fallen asleep on his bike as he'd been crossing the Nullarbor Plain. The road is quiet, and he'd fallen far enough off the road for him to have remained hidden for days. The story went that he'd knocked himself unconscious and "boiled" to death in his black bike gear. I'd met a Japanese guy in Sydney who'd told me that his plan was to ride across the centre of the continent. He'd equipped himself with a tourist map, which was probably more use as toilet paper on such a trip—it didn't even show where the cattle stations were along the way. He had just 400 kilometres of fuel range and had six litres of water capacity, plus complete confidence that he was going to make it. I'd passed on the little experience I had, with the key being that if he really was serious, then he should make sure that he took every opportunity to let someone know where he was going and when he expected to get there.

There are simple keys to travelling in the Outback and to my mind it is no more dangerous than sailing a boat, if the rules are followed. Your transport has to be in top-rate condition and you have to know how to use it properly—being able to fix problems is a major bonus. Repair stations are few and far between, though when you find one the guys can fix just about anything. You should stay on the beaten track, as if you break down, sooner or later someone will come along.

If you do have trouble, then you should stay with your vehicle. There are loads of stories about people who died because they didn't follow that rule. If you are planning to go off the beaten track, then you should tell someone responsible that you are doing so before you set off, and then you should report in when you reach your destination. Police stations, pubs, and bush stores are the perfect places to do this.

You should also carry enough food, fuel, and water to reach your destination, and to cover several days of being broken down in the bush. If you stay in the shade and do nothing, ten litres of water will last you about five days. Find out how to make a solar still to augment your water supply. If the worst happens, then don't be afraid to set fire to your oil supply, with which you've covered anything that will burn. Something slightly green will help the oil to make a good smoke cloud. Take a mirror off your bike so you can use it to flash at any airplanes. You are going to be a dot in the middle of nowhere, so you must do everything you can to be seen. If the worst comes, set fire to a tyre—that'll give you a great smoke cloud! If that all fails, then, when the day is at its coolest, collect rocks, bushes, wood, and so on. Use them to make an enormous straight line or a circle. The bush is always filled with irregular shapes, so if you make a regular shape it's highly likely to be noticed from above.

Australia is phenomenal to explore. It's a hugely diverse continent with some of the most stunning scenery in the world. Its wildlife is unique; you'll never see its like anywhere else on earth. There are challenges aplenty, but it's very easy to be lulled into a false sense of security. The Outback demands respect. You need to fire on all cylinders, all of the time. Do so and every day will be filled with surprises and adventures. When I finally made it back to the coast after the months exploring and being enthralled by the Outback, a sense of calm achievement slid over me. I'd learnt much. Sitting and staring out over the rich blues of the Pacific Ocean, I knew that I'd been gifted a set of unforgettable memories by this quirky land and its people. Inspired, I decided that home would have to wait a year or two longer for me. I would head north of Australia to explore Indonesia, the world's largest archipelago. Island-hopping through a different world and a new set of challenges awaited.

Sam Manicom has been an avid traveller from the age of 16. He's used various forms of transport, including bicycle and sail, and hitchhiked in many parts of the world. Within three months of starting to ride a motorcycle, Sam set off to travel the length of Africa. This planned one-year trip turned into eight years of adventures around the world.

He now works full-time in the world of adventure travel. When not travelling, writing, or conducting presentations, he's very much involved with travel-related organisations. In 2011, Sam joined the team of advisers working with travellers supported by The Ted Simon Foundation, and he is a co-host of the Adventure Rider Radio RAW show. In 2017, he was awarded the OVERLAND Magazine *Spirit of Adventure Award for his contribution to overlanding.*

He's been writing for magazines in the USA, Canada, the UK & Australia since 1996 and is the author of four motorcycle travel books: Into Africa, Under Asian Skies, Distant Suns (Southern Africa, & South - Central America) *and* Tortillas to Totems (Mexico, the USA & Canada).

🌐 *Sam-Manicom.com*
🐦 *@SamManicom*
📘 */AdventureMotorcycleTravelBooks*

TRAVEL IS FATAL ...

By Jacqui Furneaux

In the eighteen months I'd been travelling with my motorcycle, I had learned that it was often the near-disasters that led to the most interesting results. Under the present circumstances—having just broken my leg in a remote, mountainous part of northern Pakistan—it was difficult to see quite how.

But I wasn't dead. That was the main thing. Everything else could be sorted out.

"Travel is fatal..." begins a quote from Mark Twain, and although I was still alive, I had certainly been stopped dead in my tracks on the dirt road from Gilgit to Chitral in northern Pakistan in October 2001.

Linked with Taliban terrorism, Pakistan has a negative image. But how dangerous could it be to ride my 500cc Enfield Bullet around Pakistan with the Dutchman I'd met whilst backpacking the year before? He'd tempted me into buying my own Enfield, and together we'd followed random tracks all over India and Nepal, kissing tarmac when we'd exhausted ourselves on arduous dirt paths and then–diving off-road again. With unlimited time and no satellite navigation, we were free to follow our adventurous noses. For the first time in my life, I revelled in the excitement and freedom of not knowing where I was or where I was going.

I'd learned how to travel rough, unplanned, spontaneous, cheap, and dirty. Occasionally I had nags of guilt. What did I think I was doing riding this motorbike along beaches, through rivers, and up goat tracks in the mountains? Aimless exploring was wonderful. I'd been away from home for long enough to forget I wasn't born to do this, but ... wasn't I supposed to be working and saving for my pension or something?

Dismissing such thoughts, the day of the accident, I was riding in front on the narrow, winding track when suddenly, from a left-hand bend, a red truck hurtled towards me. With the river a steep drop below to the right and sheer mountain scree to my left, I had nothing to do but wait for the inevitable crunch. Immediately afterwards, all was still except for the tinkle of cooling metal from both vehicles. I knew my right leg was broken. I looked down and saw a bit of shin-bone sticking through my jeans; my foot was facing backwards. Rather than waiting for someone else to do it, I disengaged my ankle from the foot peg where it was impaled and turned my foot to face the front. It was to be the last act of my own decision for a long time. Hendrikus caught up with the scene and took command. My leg felt only numb at this stage—I wasn't rolling around in agony, as I thought one would with a broken bone—but Hendrikus gave me some painkillers. Then he lifted me into the back of the very truck that had run into me. Some villagers assured us they would look after the motorbikes. I was more fed up than worried. This put a sudden end to our proposed ride across the top of Pakistan from east to west before snow closed this road. BLAST!

"You go on without me," I told Hendrikus. "I'll manage." But he wouldn't hear of it and held me tight in the back of the truck to save me from the jarring of the punishing dirt track.

The man who had driven into me said, "Don't worry, Madam. Your leg is not broken."

"Your leg is broken," said the doctor at the health centre at Gupis, the village we'd ridden through ten miles back. After an injection to deal with the pain and the application of a temporary plaster, a vehicle was found which served as ambulance for me and taxi for locals cadging a ride. I was admitted to Gilgit's general hospital until I could be flown to Islamabad. I spent two nights there, watching cats catching cockroaches in my spartan room. I hadn't thought I'd be seeing Gilgit again since leaving our camping spot in the garden of the North Inn there only two days before. We'd been staying there a few weeks to work on the bikes after heavy roads and heavy loads had taken their toll.

A generous engineer had allowed us use of his workshop, tools, and expertise. There were no girlie calendars hanging on his walls. There were no hydraulic workbenches, electric tools, or inspection pits either. Just a square concrete building, part of a terrace in what Hendrikus and I called Mechanic Street, because the whole long road was lined with engineering workshops and light industry. In spite of being located in one of the most beautiful parts of the world, Mechanic Street looked grubby and ugly.

There was beauty aplenty, though. It was in the effort everyone made to overcome language and cultural differences and share the common language of engineering and just being human. After weeks of seeing me getting my hands dirty, sprawled on the floor doing maintenance on the Enfields, the locals' initial shyness at having a woman in the place had faded.

One afternoon, a man wearing traditional shalwar-kameez appeared in the workshop doorway carrying a tray, like an usherette at the theatre. What was he selling? Not choc-ices or sweets. His tray was piled with what looked like... turnips! They were small, clean, and white, with a hint of purple, and definitely turnips. Costing a rupee or two, these late-harvest delicacies were fallen upon by the thrilled mechanics. Buying a round of turnips for the mechanics was as bonding an experience as buying a pint.

We often ate at the hotel restaurant to repay their kindness for not charging us for camping on their lawn. The hotel was filling up with people arriving for the town's Silk Route Festival, a celebration of thousands of years of trading between East and West. The atmosphere in town was vibrant.

We were befriended by Bobby, one of a troupe of comedy puppeteers who were putting on a show at the festival. He was a bright and funny young man who found us amusing, too. Hendrikus and I were both sleeping in a tent made for one. Bobby called it our "mobile palace."

"Promise you will come for tea if you come to Rawalpindi," he ordered. We said we would, but that we were heading to Chitral in western Pakistan. We would have to be quick, too, as autumn was creeping up on us. Soon the mountain roads would be closed with snow for months.

One afternoon of the week-long Silk Route Festival was set aside for females only. I talked to some of the women there, who were as interested in me as I was in them. They couldn't understand why I should want to leave my home and family to go travelling in strange countries on a motorbike. For Pakistani women to travel without male relatives would be frightening and shameful, if not impossible. This overrode any desire to see more of their country.

Later, I met a tour guide who was a Taliban supporter. He told me I shouldn't believe all we hear in the West about conditions for women in Pakistan and that if he had his way, no women would be permitted to come to the festival at all. "They should stay safe at home," he insisted. Safe from whom? I wondered.

The festival wasn't only a trading exhibition with stalls; there was a fun fair and evening dance and singing performances (by and for men only). Enticing depictions on posters outside the Wall of Death motorcycle show promised thrills. Excitedly, we climbed the steps to the viewing platform and waited for the fanfare, the sense of occasion, the spectacle of a ringmaster. Instead, a bored-looking bloke strolled in wearing traditional baggy grey trousers and long shirt. A cigarette hung from his mouth. With not a vestige of showmanship, he got on a 125cc motorbike, started it up and began the ascent up the vertical wall of the wooden drum-shaped structure. Two-stroke fumes filled the air. The noise was deafening in the enclosed space. Genuinely impressed when he became horizontal and lifted his arms over his head, we clapped enthusiastically, unlike the rest of the audience, who filed out silently after the two-minute show without any reaction at all.

The festival ended; everyone went home and it was time for us to move on too. Hendrikus needed to return to Europe to earn more travel money, hence our planned westward route. We had to cross over the Shandur Pass before the snow came, or we would be stranded.

The Hindu Kush loomed ahead as we followed the mica-blue Gilgit River towards Chitral. Then the accident happened. Within minutes it all changed and everything was out of my control.

When the news got round that I was in hospital, people we'd got to know in Gilgit came to visit me. One was the chef at the hotel where we'd been camping. He had let us cook our food in his kitchen. Also came the lad from the chai shop opposite the workshop; Simon from the British Council furtively brought a very welcome bottle of whisky; and one of the mechanics came in with some milk, fresh from his cow.

Flying over the beautiful mountains in an hour—a journey which had taken us three Enfield-weeks—was almost worth breaking my leg for! In Islamabad, the orthopaedic surgeon explained that he would be fixing a locally made metal external frame around the broken bone with pins inserted into the bone-ends to hold them in place whilst they fused. After ensuring the insurance would pay for this five-star private hospital, I signed the documents and was prepped for the surgery.

After the operation, I found my leg inside the clumsy frame consisting of four metal circles joined together with struts and sturdy metal pins which went through the skin and into the bones. It was most uncomfortable and awkward. I fainted with pain when a physiotherapist made me walk. Hendrikus snarled at him. He also alarmed patients, visitors and medical staff by running with me in a wheelchair round the spacious hospital and grounds. I loved it and squealed all the way!

With this frame fitted, I was able to hobble about with crutches and there was no reason to remain in hospital. I had decided to stay in Pakistan, but the question of where to go now had to be considered. Hendrikus rang Bobby to tell him what had happened and the same day he, his brother, sister-in-law, and niece turned up with flowers, toiletries, and a demand that we stay with them. Surely this was stretching the previous invitation to call in for a cup of tea a bit far? Not only did this hospitable family give us the best bedroom in their home, they also changed their squat toilet for a sit-down European one just for me. Satisfied it was safe to leave me, Hendrikus set off on an 18-hour bus journey to fetch his bike, travelling 300 kilometres back to Gilgit and then to the village where the accident had happened. True to their word, the villagers had garaged the Enfields. Mine was not badly damaged and, and Hendrikus haggled for compensation from the owner of the 4WD. There was no vehicle insurance; matters were settled over tea. Hendrikus came back with his Enfield and enough money to cover the excess on my insurance.

Living with a Pakistani family would be interesting on any level, but living with this family was hilarious. Bobby's brother's wife and their little girl were almost as funny as the men. As the men worked all evening, they turned night into day!

In the mornings, while they slept, I hopped to the kitchen on my good leg to make tea and eat bananas and biscuits for breakfast. I washed in the tin bath in the bathroom and then sat in the garden to let the sunshine, a natural antibiotic, work on the wounds whilst trying to keep the flies off. It was the month of Ramadan, when Muslims are not supposed to eat during daylight hours. Market food stalls assembled just before dusk. Everyone awaited the signal from the mosques that they could eat, drink, and smoke until dawn the next day. This suited our nocturnal hosts who slept all day, anyway.

For a Christmas treat, I asked if we could go and get my Enfield, which was still in Gilgit. It would be cold up in the mountains, so I had some odd trousers made with one leg wide enough to cover the frame. I safety-pinned slit leggings around the pins going into the bones. My leg was still very painful and every bump excruciating, but I wanted my bike with me, so I bore the journey by bus back to Gilgit. On the return, I rode pillion, with crutches clutched in my hands as we descended the Karakoram Highway. We made good progress until halfway, when a landslide totally blocked the road. We had to stay in Dasu for three days whilst the mountain road was cleared. Lorries tailed back and a community grew on the road with fires to keep the drivers warm. A controlled explosion finally sent the bulk of the landslide tumbling into the valley below, after which workmen and engineers took pity on me (and my crutches) and manhandled the Enfield over the remaining rubble. My bike was the first vehicle across. Drivers in the miles of traffic on the other side all cheered to see us, knowing the road would be open soon.

The Karakoram Highway—not the three-lane motorway its name suggests—was deserted. Hendrikus got off the bike and sat behind me. "You drive," he said. I elevated my legs on the crash bar, and he did the foot controls as I steered. I was so happy I wept.

Christmas came and all we could find as a treat was John West mackerel fillets in mustard sauce and some bread from the Afghani bakery. On Christmas morning, we went to a park in Islamabad and sat on the grass, furtively eating our food behind a bush. It was quite the strangest Christmas dinner I've ever had.

Although foreigners and non-Muslims may buy alcohol made in Pakistan, it is so much bother to get that it is hardly worth it, although when we did, it was very well-received amongst some of our friends. But the time-consuming document hunt and somehow shameful lurking about at the alcohol outlet made it preferable to go to the Coolabah Club at the Australian High Commission where we could have a game of pool, a meal, and a glass of wine.

Hendrikus found jobs teaching IT and building websites. I was bored. One day I went on the bus to Islamabad with the notion of offering my conversational services at an English-language school. I chanced on an institute run by a native English speaker, Wendy from Yorkshire, who fell on me with open arms. She had just learned that a British colleague was unable to come, leaving her a teacher short. I explained my background was in nursing, not teaching, but she said, "You're English, aren't you? Can you start tomorrow?"

By eight o'clock the next morning, I was teaching a group of diplomats from Azerbaijan. A women's group followed, then an advanced conversation group, and some private lessons. Thank goodness for the teaching books, recordings, and teachers' manual, which meant I could read in the evening what I'd be teaching the following day. It worked very well over the five months I waited for my leg to heal.

During Ramadan, it was common to see goats on buses being taken home for fattening up. The day before the Eid celebrations, I watched as a cow had prayers said over it before its throat was cut in a garden. When I was fourteen, our biology teacher took us to an abattoir as a field trip. Now, this halal death seemed a much less stressful experience for the animal whose life peacefully ebbed away.

Due to information breakdown between the hospital and the insurance company, my outpatient treatment suddenly ceased and I was forced to return to the UK.

In the weeks they fed and accommodated us, the family we stayed with accepted only treats, saying they were grateful for the opportunity to help. Offers of payment were insulting to them. That's the way of Pakistanis.

I had such a good time, happy to have this opportunity to live and work in an Islamic country.

For me, travel was not fatal. I did not die of a broken leg. I'd read only the first three words of the quote from Mark Twain...

"Travel is fatal to prejudice, bigotry, and narrow-mindedness, and many of our people need it sorely on these accounts. Broad, wholesome, charitable views of men and things cannot be acquired by vegetating in one little corner of the earth all one's lifetime."

Mark Twain, *The Innocents Abroad*, 1869

Jacqui Furneaux had no plans to see the world on a motorbike.

With childhood burn marks still visible on her leg from her father's BSA, it would take the scorching hot English summer of 1976 for Jacqui to take to two wheels herself.

Despite her understandable apprehension about motorcycle injuries—developed during a career in nursing—once she started riding, she couldn't stop.

In 2000 she bought an Enfield motorcycle in India and rode aimlessly around Asia, Australia, New Zealand, and the Americas, finally returning to Britain with many more scars on her leg after seven years on the road.

She lives in Bristol, UK with her much-dented motorbike, still her only means of transport. Her one regret is that she's never given it a name.

She has written many articles for magazines. Her book Hit the Road, Jac! *tells the story of how a nurse in her fifties learned to manage her motorcycle on dusty roads and goat tracks, from mountains to the sea, through barren deserts to lush jungles.*

🌐 *JacquiFurneaux.com*
🐦 *@BulletJac*
📘 */JacquiFurneauxTravels*

WHAT WE LOSE,
WHEN OUR FATHERS ARE GONE

By Ian Brown

This article was originally published in The Globe
and Mail. *Reprinted with permission.*

In the *anfiteatro*, I built a small man of red rocks. This was in
the Valley of the Shells, on a remote stretch of desert between
Cafayate and Salta in northern Argentina.

It was March, when hardly anyone goes there. We were on
motorcycles, the off-road variety, four men in our late 50s trying
to cheat death in the Andes, to prove we could live forever. I had
never ridden a motorcycle before. I liked it a lot, but it frightened
me, and I often fell behind.

The *anfiteatro,* or amphitheatre, was a giant, clamshell-like
declivity carved out of the sandstone of the Andes by a stream.
The Incas used it for five millennia as a megaphone to implore
the mountains (the gods of the Incas) for rain and good fortune.
Then, in the course of 50 brief years in the 16th century, the Incan
empire was wiped out.

I was the only person in the *anfiteatro*. It made my voice
extremely loud and seemed to give me a slight New Jersey accent.
I talked to myself out loud for a while, and then, in the middle of

its open ground, in a pool of warm sunlight raying down through the top of the cavern, I built a small *inukshuk*. I don't know why.

A man, a foot high. Narrow-chested, but well-balanced. It was a little cheesy, I suppose, but seemed preferable to painting "Moron Tour" or "Starsky and Hutch" on the walls of the cave, as previous visitors had.

Then I climbed back on my Honda XR 250 and leaned my way through the rest of the Quebrada de las Conchas. I loved the way the bike's engine split the piled-up air in the narrow canyons, loved careening through my turns. Every moment demanded my full attention, which I figure is why I felt so alive. Condors hovered off the cliffs plunging down to my right. Elegant *cardón* cacti, the tallest species in the world, stood on the slopes like a crowd of dignified skeptics.

An hour and a half down the road, I spotted the others, bikes parked under a tree by a roadside restaurant. I was ordering a ham sandwich when my cellphone rang. For the first time in a week.

There was only a text, from my brother.

"Dad has died," it said, characteristically brief. "Please call."

According to the time stamp, the old man had dropped away just as I was making the *inukshuk* in the amphitheatre. Not that I put any store in that kind of thing. But a death in the family always draws out the ironies. While I was trying to cheat death, my father decided not to.

*

It wasn't a tragedy. He was 98 and wanted to die, after a life that suggested he might not, ever.

Peter Henry Brown, born Feb. 7, 1914, at Winchmore Hill in north London, Essex, was one of the indestructible war generation. He played his last game of squash at 87, lived with his first and only wife in their own house until her death at 95, and was still going to work twice a week—he was a scrap-metal broker—at 98.

People liked having him around: He never willingly wanted to embarrass anyone, wasn't pushy and was a good listener with a ready laugh and an eager interest in the news of the day—especially news that reeked of impending economic doom. He liked to be the one who read the omens first. He had lived, after all, through a stretch of history when they abounded.

Twenty minutes of rigorous calisthenics daily, without fail. His profanities were limited to *bloody* and the odd, eye-rolling *Christ!* for emphasis. After 80, he threw in an f-word more often (so did everyone) but remained even-tempered. Good with figures. Quick hands and feet (boxing, wicket keeper, flyhalf for the Saracens rugby team, a tryout for England). He only ever struck me once, after I'd been especially rude to both him and my mother; I never saw the blow coming. An affection for English tailoring and manners.

He held doors for both women and men, and wore a tie—to visit his lawyer, to birthday parties, whenever a show of respect was called for. He ate fast like a wolf (a product of three brothers, boarding school, scarcity, and the navy), but never too much. He hated pears. Two scotches a day, or rye and ginger in the summer.

He was the kind of man who had standards—of ethics and clean-
liness, especially—but no killer instinct. This made me pity him
on occasion, but he had been the pawn of the world too much to
imagine dominating it: shipped to boarding school at six, yanked
out at 16 to work in the Depression, volunteered into the Royal
Navy in his 20s, commanded in the war to do secret and dangerous tasks by nightfall on shore raids into Norway and Sweden.

He fought at the battle of Narvik, and there lost his favourite
brother, Harold, to a direct hit at sea. He kept Harold's medals—all
he had of him—a swell of loss that ran under the rest of his years.
After that, he told me once, any life at all seemed like gravy.

He was married for 55 years to a woman he wouldn't stand up
to, who frequently treated him with disdain and even contempt.
In return, he adored her and thought he was nothing without her.
That old, complicated story.

This was my father. I want to make a case for him. It isn't a
straight shot: I am his son; I have my criticisms. He was too cau-
tious and afraid to fail, too suspicious of change, too alert to the
opinions of others to be as daring as I sometimes wanted him to
be. He couldn't protect us from our marauding mother, and left
that fight to his sons. On the one hand.

On the other: He was as decent as anyone I've ever met. His rarest
trait was that he had no discernible anger. Or at least he buried it so
deeply, I only ever glimpsed it (he shouted back, once, at my taunt-
ing ma). I could not emulate him in this regard. He was the genuine
item, *a really nice guy*. He worked compulsively—not for the money,

which he didn't really care about, but because the routine made him feel necessary. Feeling necessary made his life worth living.

Eventually that wore off. Last summer, at a routine vascular checkup, a doctor found him short of breath and admitted him to hospital. The aortal valve in his heart was closing up.

A stenosis, the doctors called it: You need 2.5 centimetres for the valve to work properly, and he had 0.8. That was why he had begun "puffing," as he called it, going up stairs. The blood was backing up in his atrial chamber, leaking through his mitral valve, building pulmonary hypertension. Any one of these developments could bring on "sudden death."

"He's probably had it for 20 years," the cardiologist said. (His name was Janevski, an unmemorizable one to my English father, who honoured him simply with *Doctor.*) "If they'd caught it at 75 they could have fixed it." But at 97 "he wouldn't survive open-heart surgery to replace the valve."

My father didn't want the operation anyway. In its place, the doctor prescribed water pills, a diuretic. They made him faint and pee (incessantly), and were thus infuriating. But they kept the swelling in his leg down. He was vain enough to care about such appearances.

"How do you feel?" the doctor asked him a month later, at the follow-up.

"Pretty good," my father said, in his crisp, good-natured British way. "I had trouble breathing, but then they decided not to operate, so I presume I'm fine."

"Well, actually, that's not the case," Dr. Janevski said, and laid out the truth. The old man took it well, appreciating the honesty. The doctor gave him a year to live, what with his kidney function down to 25 per cent of what it ought to have been.

That was when he started to talk in earnest about wanting to die. The harder it was to live his life in a dignified, independent fashion, the less he wished to. That he couldn't simply switch his life off and end the charade was the greatest indignity of all.

One evening, on his way out of our house, he shook his fist at the ceiling. "I'm really mad," he shouted, "and He knows why!"

"Well," someone said, "you're going to be meeting Him soon enough. You might not want to piss Him off."

"Good point," he said. His sliver of a body shook with laughter. The sense of humour is the last thing to go.

At first, I didn't notice any change. I still dropped by for a pre-dinner scotch every other Thursday. I still fetched him Saturday mornings to do his "banking" (he refused to use an ATM, preferring the "care," as he put it, of a teller) and his shopping (a bottle of single malt).

This we followed with lunch at a restaurant. He liked going out, seeing the world, being seen. The sheer fact that he was in the game at 98 gave him pleasure. He always ordered eggs.

They didn't do them to his liking (gently poached) in the dining room at the Amica at the Balmoral Club, the retirement residence 10 minutes from my house where he had been living in a pleasant one-bedroom apartment since the death of my mother two years earlier.

That was our routine. After lunch, we headed to my house, where I helped him to the garden to read the papers (he loved a good newspaper) or upstairs to the same chair he sat in when I was a boy (it had once belonged to William Shatner, when he was a young actor in Montreal) to watch "the golf." He felt for Tiger Woods, but couldn't find it in himself to cheer for Phil Mickelson. Ernie Els, the South African, was his favourite. He often stayed for dinner too.

Sometimes we repeated the routine on Sunday, though not often. He didn't want to be a burden, and I didn't want him to be. He was a burden, of course, an obligation. Until he was no longer there to be a chore.

As deaths went, his looked like it might be a good one. But after the diagnosis, he faded in phases, and the phases began to blur together. In December, he was so short of breath the Balmoral sent him to the hospital, and he didn't leave for a week. He hated every moment. He wanted to die in his own bedroom. He arrived back home on an oxygen tank, and never came off of it. I should have known that was a sign to stick around.

*

From a distance, the raddled rocks of the Andes, under the *cardón* and *piñon* trees, resemble slabs of grilled top sirloin just this side of medium rare. Of course, it doesn't help to rhapsodize about these details on a motorcycle. On the bike, you can't let your mind wander, can't care about anything beyond your own progress—a gorgeous selfishness. You concentrate so hard that you earn your destinations.

I loved the first terror-filled 20 minutes of every day's ride, adored the inevitable gust of confidence that followed—edging faster and faster until I realized with a shock how fast I was going, how close I was to disaster, whereupon I panicked and braked again. I developed a habit of shouting "Baby!" whenever I slipped through these narrow slots of luck or when I had a close call, slithering in the dirt or bouncing off a cliff wall. *Baby!* Thrilled to be lucky.

But after the text of my father's death, even the speed of my bike couldn't stem my memory of the last time I had seen him. It had been a week earlier, 5 in the afternoon. I found him in bed under the covers, fully clothed, having a nap, or at least surfacing from the daylong nap he tended to take now.

"I don't have to go on this trip," I said.

"Not at all. I'll be fine. See you when you get back." His voice as thin as his hair. The head of care at the Balmoral had insisted we replace the double bed he had shared with my mother for nearly 60 years for one with railings that could be raised and lowered. The hospital bed was safer. He was going to die, but it was still safer.

In the new bed with its shiny rails that evening, he resembled a giant, ancient baby: his shambling thoughts, his insect arms (incessantly bruised by the mere act of living, and veins like cables), his knees and elbows (the widest parts of his limbs), the huge head, the watchful eyes, his implacable mildness. He wanted nothing. He had no complaints. He was waiting to die, impatiently. I can't imagine how lonely he was.

I had bent down to kiss him. I didn't want him to die without having done that. His beard was two days old. Washed and dressed by professionals in his lair of dying, he was unshaven more often now—unheard of when he was self-sufficient, an occurrence as rare as spotting a great auk. My earliest memory of my father is of running my hand across his scratchy furze when he came home from work at the end of the day. His beard was the armour that made him the father and me the boy. He still wore it in my mind, though he was no longer the knight he wanted to be. My dear old fallen dad.

Then I hit the rut, the bike wobbled, my rectum clamped in panic and I was back in the present—hurtling down a narrow pavement at 80 kilometres an hour in Christ-knows-where on a motorcycle, with no memory of the previous five kilometres. I decided to try to stop thinking about my father when I was on the bike. I was happy enough not to—that hadn't been my dad, really; that was what was left of him.

*

In the fall after the old man's fatal diagnosis, before we learned how fast he would fade, my brother and I drove him to Montreal, where he first landed in Canada, where he married our mother, where his four children were born and his life in austere service as our father began.

"What would you have done if you hadn't married at 40?" I once asked him.

"I would have sailed around the world."

"Yes, but after that."

"No, that's what I would have done, I would have sailed around the world for the rest of my life." His option was no family at all, many a married man's flip-side fantasy.

In Montreal, we made a tour of our collective past—our old house, his old office, his old sports club—in the hope these places would make him feel alive again. They seemed to. He had a visit with his granddaughter, who was in her first year at McGill. (He often called her from Toronto just to hear her voice, the sound of a future.) Then, the three of us, an old man and his two boys, drove to Provincetown, on the shore of Massachusetts, to visit the small hotel my brother had bought with his partner.

It was a good trip, with the sun and the sea and the sand, all the things my father had loved since he was a boy. Tim and Dad had their hair cut in adjacent chairs at a gay barbershop on Provincetown's main street: the old man's was white and sparse, fading up off his neck like a dying emperor's.

He told us that our mother was the only woman he had ever slept with. If they met in 1943, then my father was a 29-year-old virgin. By the time she divorced her first husband and married my dad, another ten years had passed. Perhaps all that helps explain his innocence, his lack of guile. Maybe it explains why he put up with her.

"Were you faithful to her?" I asked.

"Always," he said.

"And she to you?"

"I presume so."

On Sunday, as he and I were packing to drive back to Toronto, my father called from the bathroom.

"Willie, can you help me?" My childhood name.

He had been standing up too long, shaving. He swooned in my arms. I carried him to the bed. He was so light by then, 120 pounds at most, two-thirds what he had weighed in his prime.

"I need to lie down," he said. "Can you get the cover over me?"

A moment later, he was unconscious and breathing in and out like a steam press, with a gasping, clutchy noise in between—a death rattle. I figured my brother might want to say his goodbyes.

I poked my head into the dining room. "Tim. Tim. Can you come? Quickly."

He thought the old man was dying too. "It's okay, it's okay, Dad, I love you." We couldn't tell if he could hear.

One of the guests, a nurse, walked in and took his pulse. "Thready," she said. "Would you like me to perform mouth-to-mouth?"

"No, no," I said, "I'll do that."

And I did. His stubble against my inner lip as I tried to cover his mouth, the sour taste. Three, four puffs. I was trying to gently perform CPR with my left hand, as I pinched his nose with my right. His skin was as thin as onion paper.

He came to. It was slow at first. He wasn't making any sense.

"D'you think he's had a stroke?" Tim said. The implication was obvious: I had saved his life so he could become a vegetable.

Ten minutes later, my father was sitting in the breakfast room, scarfing eggs and bacon, charming the guests with tales of the war. They adored him.

We left that night, but not before a last supper of lobster rolls, corn chowder and Cape Cod clams, the old man's favourites, at Neptune on the south side, the gold September evening light spilling over the skyline of the convoluted bowl of downtown Boston. But he ate only the chowder. "I no longer have an appetite," he said. I still have the bill in my wallet.

I helped him to the men's room, returned to the table to wait. He took so long now I thought about carrying a deck of cards.

"I just don't want the conversation to stop, you know?" Tim said, glancing at the restroom door.

Then through the labyrinth of Boston to drop my brother at the airport, me driving, my brother navigating and saying what were possibly his last words to his father.

Tim: [To me] Left here. LEFT. [To our father] I may not see you again, Dad. But I love you. You're a great guy.

Me: Now where?

Tim: I love you. I may not see you again. There's nothing I can do.

Me. A large cash payment might work. WHICH WAY?

Tim: RIGHT. I always appreciated how kind you were, how great. All those vacations, and school. Now left. LEFT.

I have a photograph of the three of us on the frenzied curb of the airport, arms around each other's shoulders: Tim red-eyed, me trying to shore up the scene. But it is my father's expression that is most interesting. He wears his existence and nothing more. He knows he will not be part of our adventuring together much longer. The three of us, shimmering with the expectation of that loss.

It doesn't matter how rational the death of your father is. It is never rational enough.

In a hotel room in Utica the next morning, it happened again: The collapse, mouth-to-mouth, resuscitation, eggs and bacon ten minutes later. This time, it was just the old man and me.

And again three hours later, on a handkerchief of grass in front of the Syracuse rest stop on I-90. "You need help?" a passing fireman asked "No, he's okay, just having a spell." I brought him round again.

This time when he came to, he said: "Don't do that again." Another joke. Hilarious, really.

He sat in the car while I gassed up and phoned my brother. "What should I do? Should I take him to the hospital?"

"No! If he dies in the United States without health coverage, it'll cost us at least $30,000. Keep him alive until you cross the border, and then go to the first hospital."

Fine. We set off at 140 clicks an hour. My father fell asleep, sagging against the seatbelt. He looked dead. I'm not going to wake him up, I thought, because if he's dead, I don't want to have to lie about it intentionally at the border.

But he wasn't dead. We made Toronto. He signed his own Do Not Resuscitate order. We added a few hundred dollars' worth of nursing care to his monthly bill at the Balmoral, bringing it to $5,000 a month.

Five grand! He was paying for it out of the proceeds from the sale of their house after my mother died. At that rate, he was good for another five years, as long as he didn't need long-term care.

Looking back, I wonder if that wasn't another reason he so eagerly wanted to die. Maybe he figured his worn-out existence wasn't worth the money.

*

In the evenings in Argentina, after a day of cheating death by moto, we debated the cost of living. Dan, a thirtysomething lawyer from Toronto who was a late addition to our group, a lovely guy, was convinced selfish baby boomers like me would bankrupt his generation with our "late-in-life treatments," our heart surgeries and our cancers and our palliative care. He had a point. We need to rethink the end of life.

"Death is scary," Dan said, tucking into a grass-fed Argentine steak the size of a small footstool. "And I don't see a cultural shift to accept it. I see fewer people paying increasingly more money to the government to fund my parents' self-entitled generation's losing battle against death."

"Oh, okay," I said. "If I get cancer, instead of trying to cure it, I'll just lie down and die, so you and your pals can have an easier go."

But what I was thinking about were my own Saturday-afternoon conversations with my father at the end, as I limped him off to lunch and a beer.

"Why can't I just die?" he often asked. He had been complaining about all the "tablets" he was suddenly taking, after never taking a pill in his life: Tylenol (he was convinced it helped him sleep), furosemide (the diuretic for his legs and heart), Senokot (bowels), Restoril (to sleep, but not so good for depression or bad kidneys or glaucoma, all of which he skirted), mirtazapine (for anxiety and to stimulate his appetite), Cosopt (eyes). "I can't understand why God would make me live like this, in such a pathetic manner."

"Yes, God can be thoughtless that way." I tried to change the subject. "What do you think will happen after you die?"

He looked at me as if I were an especially elemental form of excrescence. "I presume I'll see your mother again in heaven, of course." Pause. "And that she'll be quite put out that I've kept her waiting." A smile.

We struggled into our chairs at the restaurant table with the usual complicated hydraulics—lifting, pulling, all the while pretending it was nothing, a breeze. Then, again: "Why can't I just take a pill to die?"

"Because it's illegal."

Or one day in the hallway of the Balmoral just before Christmas, before they threaded him full-time into a portable oxygen tank, his final millstone:

"The ladies"—the women in the residence, who outnumbered the men ten to one—"say there's a way it can be done. There's a machine. You're a journalist, surely you know someone who could arrange it?"

He was referring to a morphine drip, used on young and old terminal patients alike, in palliative situations: The steady infusion of morphine decreases pain and eases anxiety but also naturally suppresses the breathing, until breathing is no longer required. The trouble was, he wasn't terminal. Well, he was—we all are, of course—but not in the way he had to be to qualify for such a contraption of mercy.

"If he doesn't have cancer," the palliative-care counsellor explained when I inquired, "he wouldn't be considered terminal."

"But he is terminal."

"The time of his death cannot be predicted with any precision."

Here is what my father hated most about the final shrivelling of old age: The involuntary drip of saliva out of the right side of his mouth. Peeing into a hand-held urinal in his chair because he couldn't get to the bathroom fast enough. Insomnia – he often called me at 5 in the morning after a sleepless night, frantic with panic. Not being able to walk, much less run. Losing weight. Losing his eyesight. Losing my mother. Not driving. Not gardening. And going to the toilet.

"If I learned that I was going to die at 2 pm tomorrow," he said to me a year before he expired, "that would be fine, because then I wouldn't have to go to the toilet again."

"Going to the toilet is so bad?"

"At my age, going to the toilet is like single-handedly planning the invasion of D-Day."

Here are a few of the things he still enjoyed: A whisky (sometimes two) with a companion. Surprise visits from people he liked. Any conversation about the news. His beloved daughters (my twin sisters). A fresh shirt and blazer and tie. His friend, Mrs. D.—she lent him espionage novels, a late discovery.

His care worker, Magnolia, who could get him out of bed, washed and dressed, in 20 minutes. Flirting with younger women (in their 50s and 60s) at parties. Fresh fruit. Any television sport requiring hand-eye co-ordination. Thinking about my mother and her sisters, his first close female friends. Gardens and flowers—the last ones he saw were some purple crocuses I wheeled him past two weeks before he died, before I left to try to feel alive again on a motorcycle.

As he grew physically weaker, his famous emotional self-control atrophied as well. He took to yelping, "Oh God, take me now!" as I cantilevered him into his chair in restaurants, a rare turn as a drama queen. The outbursts were followed by apologies—"I'm sorry to be like this, so hopeless"—which were in turn followed by long shattering bouts of silent sobbing.

By the end, it was happening at every meal, before the main course arrived. He could do everything on his own, and then he couldn't, whereupon he wanted his life to end. He wasn't what you would call sentimental.

The point is that he wanted to die sooner, but none of us could let him—not his family, not the home, not the system, not his body. End-of-life is an impressive management concept, but it's people who die, and people we hang onto. When he was finally feeble enough that he qualified for palliative care—when he was sufficiently weakened that he could do nothing on his own, and all his needs could be met in his own room—only then could he die at home, mostly at his own expense.

A patient who dies of organ failure near the end of his or her life goes for an average of $39,947. Frailty's cheaper ($31,881), but sudden death is the bargain: $10,223. I worked out once that my father's nine days in hospital and month's worth of part-time palliative care cost even less, less than $10,000 – $172 for each of the 58 years he lived in Canada. That would have pleased him.

There is a picture of him in Rockport, Mass., off the tip of Cape Ann, where he took us every summer for years: He's holding my brother and me high in his arms, in the crook of each elbow—the strong man, so proud of his little, happy boys (he is 44; we are 4 and 2). He is wearing Black Watch plaid swim trunks, and what hair he has—he was already balding in his 30s, taking after his father—is still black. The sun he loved is shining everywhere in that picture: "All the sunshine has gone out of the house," he wrote to my mother whenever she went away.

It's my brother's favourite picture of him, "how I still think of him in my mind."

His hands were huge. He kept his mother's Book of Common Prayer in his top drawer. He knew all the words to "If You Were the Only Girl in the World, and I Were the Only Boy." His all-time favourite breakfast treat was white bread fried in bacon drippings. The advice he repeated most often to me was "stay clean." My mother was the love of his life.

These are a few of the details I remember. There are many others. A man's mother fills his heart for the first time. If he's lucky, his father fixes his compass.

*

The landscape of northern Argentina is huge. Hiking on foot or bike or horse, you travel all day in the same stretch of valley, its vista unchanging. But 50 kilometres on a motorcycle slip by in an hour.

We rose at 7 a.m. to a clean light and the sound of dogs barking, ate a light breakfast and rode off into nowhere. We saved our feasts for the end of the day: meat, meat, more meat, meat and cheese, cheese, cheese and meat, and maybe a little ice cream, possibly with cheese. The average Argentine consumes 55 kilos of meat a year, plus cheese. The fact that anyone actually defecates in Argentina is a miracle.

Our final destination was Ngatzi Bay, a villa on the outskirts of ancient Salta, where the Incas once gathered gold. The villa was owned by a Rhodesian, one of South America's busiest tobacco brokers. Separate sleeping houses of African design dotted a slope down to a vast and beautiful man-made lake. A pair of parrots lived in a cage. The wife's side of the family had been tea growers in Malawi.

"I could sit all day looking at that," my friend Ben said the evening we arrived. We were out on one of the vast verandas hovering over the lake, watching *pejerrey* fishermen turn on their bait lights against a Turner evening sky and a backsplash of steep green mountain. "Paradise."

"Yes," I said. "Almost." I hoped my father had such a view, wherever he was now. Or at least I wished he could see it. I have these primitive thoughts sometimes. The other day a robin stopped in its tracks and stared at me for the longest time, chirped and stared again. I thought: It could be him, that robin—sturdy, well-dressed, forthright but unaggressive, an energetic hopper.

You miss your mother in a different, more dramatic way: You were ripped from her body, after all, and so when she dies, a part of what was once you disappears for good. But your father stands apart, watching, the one who shows you how life works, who provides context—your instructor, your guide, your tracker, your friend (if you're fortunate, and I was) and finally your companion. Eventually, if things go the way they are supposed to, he leaves before you do and you face the world without the person who first ventured it beside you.

What he leaves is a gap, a fissure in your belief that the world is worth exploring. It doesn't feel like much at first, especially if he was a good father, because he's made you believe you don't need him. That is the job of the father, after all—to fail his children, gently.

When he finally died at 11:30 that morning, as I flew through the mountains of northern Argentina on the back of a quivering motorcycle, my father had been in bed for two days. He had stopped eating: If he couldn't get the morphine drip, he was going to do it himself. He had always been able to rely on his body. My wife, my brother and my brother's partner had had a few laughs with him the night before he went. I had spoken to him by telephone two nights earlier, but it wasn't the same.

He died quietly, with no gasping, in semi-slumber, just as he wanted it, in the company of two women who took care of him at the home.

"He was ready to go," Marlene Dixon, the head of care, told me a week later. "And he wanted to go. And he just let go. I think he was at peace with that." She said a few more things. Then she said, "He saw himself as more and more of a burden as he declined. 'I don't want to be a bore,' was how he put it." Her own father had died three decades earlier, at 69, when she was 21. She spoke of it as if it had happened the day before.

*

It took me five days to get back from the middle of nowhere, by which time my siblings from New York, Denver and Chicago had gathered. The funeral was gracious. The wake was pleasant. We'll scatter him in the North Sea, where he can at last join my mother off the coast of Suffolk, where they first met and were once so happy. I don't feel sad too often, but I find myself unexpectedly driving by his place on my bike or in the car—the place where I saw and held and loved him, rather than his memory.

A few days later, I went by to fetch his notebooks, the ones with everyone's phone numbers repeated anew every few pages, the props he used to maintain the routine of a normal life until he couldn't pretend any more. I was on my way out again when I ran into Scholastique, the Congolese nurse who had administered to my father as he weakened. She said she was sorry. "But for everyone, one day has to be the last day."

I agreed, and thanked her, and stepped onto the slowest elevator on Earth for the last time. There I found Mrs. Cassels, another resident of that strange place, a tall, very pretty woman in her 80s. My dad had talked about her: He said she was a first-rate golfer, and rumoured among the residents to be from a vast pile of old Toronto money. Old money always fascinated my Pa—he wanted to know if it made all the difference the old-money types claimed it did.

"You're Mr. Brown's son," Mrs. Cassels said.

I said I was.

"How's your Dad?"

"He died," I said. "About a week ago."

"Oh," she said, alert but not surprised. "Oh! He was great! He had lovely English jackets."

"Yes," I said. "Yes, he did."

Ian Brown is well-known for his work on TVO and CBC Radio, where he was the moderator of Talking Books *for more than a decade, and also hosted* Sunday Morning *and* Later the Same Day. *He is the author of four books:* FreeWheeling, *which won the National Business Book Award;* Man Overboard; The Boy in the Moon, *which was chosen by the New York Times as one of the ten best books of 2011; and, most recently,* Sixty, *shortlisted for the Taylor Prize. His work has been published in eight countries.*

ON A MISSION TO THE MISSION

By Lisa Morris

Anyone who knows me well knows that the thought of sand riding sends cold shivers down my spine. It penetrates my every cell and seems to scatter molecules beyond the boundaries of my own skin. In the dark depths of my mind, I wanted to think my sand days were safely behind me, buried like nuclear waste in airtight containers.

"Why, pray tell, can't I stay in first gear?" I enquired hopefully, en route to the Misión San Francisco de Borja, a Spanish mission located in Baja California. "I like first gear. We get on and I feel a lot more in control," I continued, conscious of concealing any "princess tendencies" from my argument. Jason's expression told me he wasn't buying what I was selling. "Second gear is a tad too fast for me, and I can't give it handfuls of gas in first," I persevered, instantly regretting not having voiced such thoughts in the safety of my head first.

Jason had countered with a razor-sharp rationale tens of times already, and did so again Namely, over-revving the engine in "snatchy" first gear prevented me from going a notch faster on sand when I needed to regain balance. Of course he was right, and the subsequent silence hung in space.

An idea struck me that was so far out I had to repeat it to myself. After I had, it seemed even more outrageous. It stemmed from a

Zen story about the villages of Khun Yuam, a small district in northern Thailand, where the locals occasionally ensnare mon keys. (Presumably for an entertaining distraction rather than dinner.) The narrative delves into how the villagers chain a ewer—a bulbous-bottomed pitcher with a wide spout—to the base of a tree. They fill the container's base with nuts and other foodstuffs appealing to primates. Overnight, a monkey ventures over and slips his hand down the narrow neck, grabbing the loot in hand while making a fist. That means it's now too big to get back up the slender neck, and he's trapped.

The point being: If you want to be free, all you have to do is let go. Its meaning struck a chord with me, partially because when let loose on rough terrain, I do tend to over-clench my handlebar grips—the left one has been worn down smooth. It was time to go with it. If I could stay enlightened to that, it might just lead to "Slowly, slowly, catchee monkey." Fear now ring-fenced, I threw my leg over Pearl, my trusted BMW F650GS, and got going.

A crimson ball of sun rose over the eastern horizon. Streamers of orange light fanned out across the clear blue sky before spilling over the land in a deluge of amber. We were leaving the ocean behind, and a ribbon-like highway seemingly tossed into the rocks revealed itself; the sun glinted off of it, flecking an otherwise dry and dusty desert.

After dodging a swarm of oncoming 4WDs, we branched off the blacktop and onto the dirt track, immersing ourselves in a boojum-laden landscape where cacti like inverted hairy carrots twisted and turned skyward. Careering like wobbling Jell-O over a half-mile of silky sand, I managed to get Pearl onto the rocky road unscathed.

The scenery intensified. If the desert was the monochromatic start of an old black-and-white film, the landscape had turned to Technicolor. Amid a verdant landscape of saturated greens, the cacti glowed against the afternoon light, so richly that it made the setting look like it had been cooked on a black-light version of Photoshop. It curbed my concentration every throttle twist of the way and instead, forced me to be mindful while weaving through such visual splendour.

It was a song of an off-road route. The floor invited me to dance to a rhythm of compacted dirt, manageably jagged stones, and a light smattering of sand. Mercifully, there were only a few rocks bigger than a tennis ball thrown in for amusement. Pearl hesitated not a second in jolting my muscle memory, enabling me to slip back into a groove of sorts. As we embraced the lumps and bumps together, she seemed certain of the first step in her lead. I felt alive by my motorcycle's flair for emboldening me to take the reins in wielding her with artful precision. She's the underdog as much as a dark horse, that one.

The afternoon passed perfectly. Though riding somewhere close to my technical limits, I was in a heady frame of mind, buoyed up by skimming the sand as opposed to drowning below its surface, buzzing at every curve ball thrown my way.

Then bedlam erupted. "Oh my giddy ants! What the...?" came unbidden from my lips seconds after cornering a blind bend. An oncoming dirt biker sped towards me in my lane, oblivious that anyone besides him and his crew might also be enjoying the trails I reluctantly shared a disturbing moment with the guy: no margin for his error and nowhere for me to go ... this was going to hurt. Too stunned to honk my horn, I watched helplessly as the goggled guy barely changed his line of direction, squeezing around me like whitewater diverging around a rock, leaving only a hair's breadth to spare. Too close for comfort, chap—be a dear, and switch lanes.

That's the problem with luck, it can run out at any hairy moment. A trio of dry, rocky riverbeds—encompassing stones the size of rugby balls—stood between the mission and me. "Okay, here we go!" I cried, as Pearl bobbled over rocks ricocheting off her boulder basher. Uncharacteristically, I gave it my all. Without even thinking about it I got into a flow, throwing my wheels this way and that, slaloming through bundles of rocks, sending up clouds of fine dust, and closing fast on the finish line.

Having precariously zigzagged a rockbound course, I dismounted my bike. "We've made it," I mused, pleased and perspiring. Having removed my glove, I could see the spike of my pulse, heightened by adrenaline, coursing through my hand. I found myself shaking like a leaf and laughed incredulously. A mind-blowing 22 miles of wending our way on an undulating, curling track had eventually led us to our destination.

Jesuit missionary Wenceslaus Linck officially founded the mission in 1762, and the knowledge that this region (traditionally referred to as Ádac by the Cochimí Indians) had a potable source of water was all the impetus the priests needed to begin formal construction. The funds were provided by the Duchess of Gandía, a member of the famous House of Borgia, hence its name.

From its humble beginnings as a small Jesuit outpost for the nearby Misión Santa Gertrudis de Cadacamán, in its heyday the Misión San Francisco de Borja administered to a booming community of nearly 2,000 converts. After the expulsion of the Jesuits in the mid-18th century due to false speculation around wealth they allegedly kept from the Spanish king, the Franciscans waltzed in and took charge for five years. Their legacy was a sizable adobe mission church. When responsibility was transferred to the Dominicans in 1772, they erected a stunning cut-stone church in front of the adobe one. This is the church I now saw before me.

The mission was abandoned in 1818 due to the indigenous population being decimated by the introduction of European disease—there was simply no one left to proselytize to.

As postage stamp-sized places go, the view was phenomenal. A necklace of rough-hewn constructions are dotted around achingly off-white structures, the outlying mission buildings and ruins that have survived, perforating the cactus gardens and thick desert vegetation. Today's custodians of the mission are comprised of just one family (headed by caretaker José Gerardo), a paddock of working horses, a small herd of goats, two charming little dogs pining for food and affection, and scores of howling coyotes on the periphery.

Not a single cloud adorned the bright sky. As the sun traversed westward on its afternoon journey, shadows stalked across the mission. Bands of burnt orange and pink gathered to greet an early dusk. Toads serenaded me, putting out their croaking clicks and groans. A few pale stars scattered themselves and twinkled across a bruise-coloured horizon, their light hugging the heavens. I swung gently from my hammock beneath the palapa and watched the mission settle in for the night.

Supernovas exploded and collapsed overhead, punching holes in the galaxy before luminously retreating into the next world. Here below, on an earth night humming with desert critters, I glimpsed a falling star streak the sky. It was that sort of place, that sort of night. Jason's face sailed quietly across the dark oceans of sleep, lit by a soft glow spilling from the moonlight.

I emerged into the new day astride Pearl with enough hubris on the first stretch of sand to believe I could do this. I knew not where such an exaggerated pride or unearned self-confidence came from—perhaps the tectonic plates of my universe were shifting, having taken a giant leap of faith. More likely it came from my plucky old bike. I didn't dare look back lest to give myself a fright from whence I came.

"Rockeee AND sandeee!" Jason chanted down the intercom to keep my mood and motorcycle maneuvering light. "Mr. Sandman, bring me a dream..." I sang in response, through a shower of sand. I ran the sight of it through my mind once more to ensure my longing to ride sand hadn't monkeyed my vision. Only then did I surrender to emotion, unchain my feelings, and let my heart soar.

During a handful of small sections, the path oscillated between loose and compacted ground, then gave way to thickening sand, with no signs of relenting for about a mile. I could feel the intense concentration written on my face. I hadn't catapulted or capitulated, which was comforting. Sure, I was more wooden spoon than gold medal, but between one heartbeat and the next, I fishtailed down the trail. I have to admit, I was amped.

Jason's F800GS fared not so well. He had pushed his luck by letting the drone battery for his aerial photography system suck the life force from the motorcycle battery, and the former had left the latter worse for wear. Namely, the bike failed to start every time it died or he turned the ignition off. Jason dropped his bike once, and started it up with the support of mine; again it happened, same drill, and thrice on repeat. His riding style was comparable to Russian roulette that morning: a stop-start game that left Jason down and out before he even had the chance to start playing.

The bike took a beating, as did Jason—parched and panting under an unyielding sun. Vertically challenged legs straddling a tall, quarter-tonne weight on a narrow front wheel gave him little traction, let alone much leverage to save the bike from toppling. Rather, his energy was swiftly sapped each time he summoned enough strength to push the laden leviathan back up. Coolant started to leak everywhere. I took a moment to think—the remainder of this sortie was going to be a roll of the dice, that was for sure.

Squelching in his suit, wet with sweat, Jason knew he had made an error a trained monkey would have avoided: putting Captain Slow in front, letting me assume an unbending snail's pace. Unhurried speeds were always a no-go for Jason, and I suspect for all other competent sand riders. Despite the fact I thought I was going quite fast, harbouring a newfound respect for sand in second gear, my doubts began to resurface.

We pressed on, determined to see this thing out. "Lisa, you're riding like an absolute pro today; I can't believe you don't need any persuasion. I'm so proud of you," Jason said in a voice freighted with kindness. As his spirited words continued, I wanted to grab handfuls of them out of the air and stuff them into my mouth, feeding off them like a praise-led pubescent. Happy emotions swirled around me; smiling widely, I was at risk of swallowing my own ears.

In a sudden reality check, I felt my arms tense up. I was about to lose control in a drift of sand. Jason intervened, "Look ahead! Look where you want to go and the bike will follow." Fighting a tumult of spiralling thoughts, I rallied, kept going, and staved off any fissions of fear. The best white-knuckle ride of my life ensued.

After my enlivening Mexican cocktail of pitching over washboard corrugations, yawing through pillowed sand and watermelon-sized rock, I was present, perhaps for the first time all day. The moment was extraordinary. I realised that if I took my last breath soon I would have known this, a connection with my life, with all of its errors and cockeyed, unconventional successes.

Deep in endorphin-fuelled euphoria, a feeling like no other came with getting the hang of sand, washing away my fear. I was not yet quite able to revel in sand, but if nothing else, we were no longer archenemies. Some inroads had been made in making amends; for all I knew, we had even begun to bond.

Sweat-drenched and spent, I catalogued the day's adventures against the untold possibilities ahead. My plateaued riding ability now abated, I took pleasure in knowing that, today at least, I had graduated *magna cum laude*.

Born and bred in Great Britain, Lisa Morris has sunk into various continents over the last two decades—instructing and co-running scuba diving trips around the watery globe with her partner, Jason Spafford. They are currently wending their way around the Americas on two wheels. Lisa is a spirited advocate for women riders and adores telling tales on the trails for various motorcycle, overland, and travel publications. Jason meanwhile engages his passions as an adventure travel, underwater and wildlife photographer, drone pilot, filmmaker and stock footage producer.

🌐 *TwoWheeledNomad.com*
▪️ */twowheelednomad*
◉ *@TwoWheeledNomad*

THE END OF THE WORLD AS WE KNOW IT

By Jordan Hasselmann

The plan was simple enough, or so we thought. We'd spent a couple of days recovering, eating, drinking and getting cleaned up after our eight-day hike of the Torres del Paine "O" Circuit, and now it was time to get moving again. We set our course for Punta Arenas, where we'd catch a ferry to cross the Strait of Magellan to Tierra del Fuego, about 250 kilometres further south.

It was a warm and sunny day and we anticipated a perfect day for riding. We'd heard that southern Chile and Tierra del Fuego in particular could be a bit windy, but we're from the Canadian prairies, so we thought were familiar with wind. A minus-40°C Winnipeg winter wind at the corner of Portage and Main can teach you everything you need to know about wind. At least that is what we'd been led to believe.

We were so naive.

Everything seemed completely normal as we left town; however, that all changed as we rounded the first bend and were slammed by an invisible force so strong that it nearly pulled us out of our saddles. We were both blown over the yellow line and clear across the road. Luckily there was no oncoming traffic. And that is how things went for the rest of the day—we fought the wind constantly, leaning our bikes as far over as we could to keep them going in a straight line. Half way to Punta Arenas, there is a large "Monument to the Wind" sculpture, but we did not stop to pay our respects.

At least we had some company along the way. There was hardly any traffic, but the fields were filled with wild guanacos (the llama's bigger, more graceful and undomesticated cousins), sheep, and rheas. Rheas are large flightless birds like emus and ostriches. They look exactly like massive feather dusters. At least the guanacos had the decency to keep their distance. The rheas, on the other hand, were running all over the place, including across the road in front us. Actually, we couldn't tell if they were running across the road or being blown across—either way, they can move pretty fast!

We arrived in Punta Arenas to find yet another surprise. Since we had spent the last eight days in the Chilean backcountry around Torres del Paine without access to any news, we did not know that Punta Arenas had suffered a massive river flooding only days before.

We were exhausted from the ride, so we didn't notice much at first, then as we neared the town centre we could see the roads and parks were covered in a sea of mud. Thankfully the cleanup was already well underway; however, many streets were impassable. Some shops and houses were completely engorged with more than a metre of solid mud on the main level. The streets that were open were slick with a heavy layer of incredibly slippery river mud, so we tiptoed our way through emergency vehicles and cleanup crews and eventually made it to our hostel.

We didn't sleep much that night. Not because we shared a dorm room with four other travellers (and one who needed to investigate the contents of her crinkly plastic bags a surprising number of times during the night), but because the intense winds outside rattled the windows, shook the house, and howled all night long. When we woke, the winds were still going strong.

Despite the winds, we packed up and headed out. As we drove to the end of the block, the wind seemed to be manageable. When we turned the corner and left the protection of the buildings that lined the street we'd been on, we felt its full wrath. As we pulled away from a streetlight, the wind blasted us, knocking Sandra and her motorcycle to the ground. I barely made it across the intersection.

I pulled over and ran back to help her pick up the bike and as I made my way back to my bike, I could see the tire tracks I had left in the mud-coated street. Because of the extreme wind, I had actually left diagonal tracks in the mud with both my front and rear wheels. I didn't even know that was possible. We rode directly back to the hostel, unpacked and stayed another night. Total distance travelled: one kilometre.

We checked the wind report when we got back to the hostel: 91 kph (49 knots, 57 mph).

That explained a lot.

Things were slightly better the next morning, and we made the decision to leave. Patagonia is famous for its wind and it certainly was living up to its reputation; however, we still needed to get off the mainland and reach the island of Tierra del Fuego. There are two ferries that will take you to Tierra del Fuego; from Punta Arenas it is a two-hour ride aboard the main ferry across the Straits of Magellan, or you can drive 160 kilometres northeast and take a smaller (and free) ferry which crosses at a much more narrow spot, therefore running every 20 minutes. Since the big ferry wouldn't be leaving until 5 pm, we chose the latter.

The road took us along the north shore of the Strait of Magellan until we reached the ferry station, and our timing was perfect. The last cars and trucks were just boarding the landing craft-style ship, and we were directed just to ride up the ramp. Easier said than done. The ferry more or less runs aground and drops a ramp to load and unload cars, and in the wind the waves were moving the ship around like crazy and making it a moving target.

Once aboard, the short crossing was extremely rough, so we stood beside the bikes, holding on to them tightly in an attempt to prevent them from falling over while the ferry rolled and pitched excessively. It was a long 20 minutes.

Once we were successfully across, we found a spot for lunch and considered our options. It was getting on in the day and we still had a couple of hundred kilometres to cover as well as a border crossing into Argentina. There were two gravel roads heading out of the small town of Cerro Sombrero, both of which would take us where we wanted to go. We talked to some fellow diners in the restaurant about which would be a better choice for us and our motorbikes. One man said the western route was better, one said the eastern route was better, and one reported that both roads were equally terrible. We decided to take the route our GPS device recommended—a decision we would soon regret.

The first three or four kilometres were manageable, but it was all downhill from there. We soon learned that the GPS had put us on the main trucking route. There was not a lot of traffic, but what little there was took the form of huge semi-trucks that hogged the entire road, showering us with stones. The road was full of huge ruts created by the trucks that would grab our tires and throw the bikes around. However, what made it even more treacherous were the long stretches of deep gravel that would arrive without notice, causing the bikes to change direction unexpectedly and shaking the handlebars violently from side to side. This type of riding would have been unpleasant but manageable under normal conditions, but by now the wind had become ferocious, further complicating matters.

So in addition to fighting the road and avoiding trucks, we also had to fight the wind by leaning our bikes into it with all of our strength at quite frankly ridiculous angles in an attempt to keep going in a more or less straight direction. This caused the bikes to slide around even more in the deep gravel. The wind pushed us straight across the road to the edge of the opposite ditch on numerous occasions.

Under these conditions there are two options: stop and pull over or go faster. Slowing down in deep gravel almost guarantees an accident. Since we were in the middle of nowhere, stopping was not really an option, and besides, we would have surely been run

over by a semi-truck minutes later. Reluctantly, we chose option
number two and opened the throttle as much as we dared. I can't
count the number of near-misses, last-minute saves, and almost-
crashes we survived, but it was without a doubt the most difficult
and scariest ride of our entire trip. Two hours later, we arrived at
the Argentinian border, exhausted, sore, and extremely proud!

There were still a few hours of daylight left, so we decided to
push on to the town of Rio Grande, another decision we'd soon
regret, but for different reasons.

The Argentinians seem to be obsessed with the Falkland Islands,
or the Malvinas as they call them, and since this was the 30th
anniversary of the war against the British, Malvinas banners and
commemorative celebrations were everywhere, including in Rio
Grande, headed up by the populist president, Cristina Fernández
de Kirchner.

It was late in the day; we were frozen, exhausted, and emotion-
ally drained. However, because of the celebrations there were no
available hotel rooms in the city, and it was just too cold and windy
to camp. We rode around to 10 or 12 hotels and hostels; all of them
were full. We asked hotels to call other hotels, to no avail. This was
the first time during our trip that we had had a problem finding a
place to stay. We never made reservations—we just showed up and
someone had always found room for us.

Finally, after two hours, one innkeeper eventually found a hotel
for us. Sadly, it was in a large luxury hotel at a cost of approximately
ten times what we usually pay for a night's lodging. Reluctantly

we pulled out our credit card and called it a night. After such an eventful day it was actually pretty nice to have a night of luxury, so maybe it was not all bad.

The next day we got up, topped the bikes up and rode the final 300 kilometres to Ushuaia, the most southerly city in the world. The further we went, the more scenic the landscape became. From flat pampas to rolling hills to dramatic mountains, the scenery on Tierra del Fuego kept getting better and better. As we crossed the final mountain pass, we could feel the excitement rising. After nine months on the road we'd be reaching the actual end of the road—you literally can't go any further.

Reaching Ushuaia is a special moment for all overland travellers travelling south through the Americas, and it was no different for us. It was very exciting.

Of course, we were immediately stopped by the police, who welcomed us to their city. After a quick hello, we followed the road that goes through town and out again to the end of the road. With frozen fingertips, we happily posed in front of the sign thousands of overland cyclists, motorists, motorcyclists, and personal friends had posed in front of before us.

Jordan and Sandra Hasselmann left their home in Calgary, Alberta in 2011 for a 14-month motorcycle trip of the Americas, from Calgary to Ushuaia (via Newfoundland) and back. They visited 15 countries and travelled more than 47,000 kilometres on their trusty, but somewhat

beat-up, BMW F650GSes. They have since made subsequent motorbike trips all over western Canada, as well as to the Yukon and Alaska.
Although Jordan had been riding for a number of years prior to the
trip, Sandra learned to a ride a motorcycle specifically for the trip to
Tierra del Fuego and left for South America with very few kilometres
under her belt. In addition to riding motorbikes, Jordan and Sandra
are enthusiastic travellers, hikers, skiers, snowshoers, and backpack-
ers. They try to spend as much time as possible exploring the world
beyond their front door.

   Both Jordan and Sandra were born and raised in the "heart of the
heart of the continent," Winnipeg, Manitoba, Canada. They have lived
in Alberta since 2004, and are currently planning their next adventure.

STONES IN MY PASSWAY: AN OFF ROAD JOURNEY THROUGH CAPE BRETON

By Zac Kurylyk

When I plan a motorcycle trip, I'm hoping for good roads, good scenery, and the chance to explore new territory. I'm also hoping to avoid a few things: bad weather, mechanical problems, and getting lost.

In 2014, I took a journey that delivered everything I wanted and everything I didn't want, too. But the trip worked out; my bike and I survived, and I learned to appreciate the rare occasions when everything goes right, but also the more common scenarios when everything goes wrong and something good still comes out of all the mess.

Ask motorcyclists about must-ride areas in Canada, and they usually mention Cape Breton. The Cabot Trail around the top of the island is a great ride; the curvy bits are mostly well paved, and there are fantastic views. There's plenty of other good street riding on the island as well, whether you want scenic straights or twisty back roads.

But in 2014, I was more curious about off-road riding. When my dad had lived in Cape Breton in the 1980s, he'd gone deer hunting in the Highlands, and he'd told me about an extensive gravel road system there. I asked the local adventure-riding community for more details, but couldn't find much information on the area. The best solution was to investigate for myself, which was how I ended up aboard a Beta 498 RR motorcycle, motoring madly towards the Canso Causeway, the gateway to Cape Breton.

I'd borrowed the motorcycle from the distributor so I could write a riding review. It was Beta's flagship enduro at the time, a highly-strung off-road race bike with minimal additions to make it street legal. You couldn't find a worse motorcycle to go touring on. The 498 RR was only 236 pounds without fuel, so I weighed almost as much as the bike; after adding luggage, it was a tippy combination on the freeway. At high, constant RPM, the engine delivered punishing vibration through the frame and handlebars. This machine was not aimed at the long-distance touring market, but I reckoned my choice would pay off once I hit the unpaved roads.

I was cold when I arrived at Cape Breton after a day-long ride through back roads in unseasonably chilly temperatures. I'd already made an emergency stop to tighten my chain when it started slapping against the frame (a shortcoming the local dealership had missed when they'd serviced the bike the day before). I was four hours behind schedule, and it was starting to rain. But I had a load of camping gear and a street-legal dirt bike: I figured I could handle what the wilderness dished out. I headed up the island's coast towards Judique, where I left the tarmac and started down the island's extensive system of interior unpaved roads and snowmobile trails.

Aside from the sprinkles of rain, this was exactly what I had been looking for. I rode for miles down open gravel tracks with a combination of tight corners and fast straights with good sightlines. The scenery could have been a bit better (monoculture softwood plantation isn't anyone's idea of a postcard), but for the most part, I was going too fast to care. And then, instead of having to pitch my tent in the damp underbrush, I found a snowmobile clubhouse, unlocked and dry. I was inside and warm. I even had cell reception. So what if there was a rogue rodent noisily gnawing at the wall inches from my ear? Life was good.

Little did I know what awaited me the next day.

Saturday started with a quick rip through the hills, down dirt roads surrounded by hardwood trees, blueberry fields, and old homesteads. Once, this area had been full of Scottish settlers fleeing the Highland Clearances; they were long gone now, but traces of their old road system remained. Although I'm a bit of a bumbling rider in the dirt, the Beta's raw power and supple suspension made the ride pure joy. Despite the previous day's minor mishaps, the trip was a roaring success, until halfway up a mountainside, when I unwittingly took a wrong turn on a poorly marked snowmobile trail.

Although major junctions are well-marked on Cape Breton's snowmobile routes, sometimes you run across an unmarked fork and are left wondering which way to go. Confronted with such a choice, I made the wrong guess and headed off into unknown, unmapped territory.

The trail narrowed and soon disappeared into a long, muddy water crossing, where a family of beavers had dammed off a stream and flooded the road. I knew immediately this would be a bad place to get stuck. From the lack of tracks around me, it seemed help would be a long time coming, and I really didn't want to spend my weekend hiking down to civilization in a pair of muck-filled motocross boots.

I didn't want to attempt the crossing without backup, but my other option was to turn around and risk running out of fuel in the middle of the woods, where I hadn't seen another vehicle for hours. This would mean the end of my weekend's exploration, and that was unacceptable. I was too curious about what lay ahead to turn back now, so I decided to press on and tackle the mudhole myself.

The water wasn't deep, but the bottom was pure ooze, and I bogged the front wheel axle-deep into the muck. After plenty of muscle work, I managed to bull the bike out of the filth and back onto dry gravel. I assessed my situation: I was in rough shape. I was soaked and filthy from wrestling the bike out of the hole, still running low on gas, still on the wrong side of the mudhole, and now the bike wouldn't start.

I hit the electric start—no luck. I tried the kick-starter; the only reward was a bruise on my shin from the footpeg. I checked the wiring harness, and nothing seemed wet. I was just out of luck, in the middle of the woods.

Beta includes a top-notch toolkit on their bikes, so I drained the carb and checked the intake. All was good—no flooding—and after a few minutes the bike started up easily. When I checked the crank-case, though, I saw that water had somehow made its way into the bottom end. The gears were coated with milky, polluted oil.

I was in a jam. Not only was I stuck, with no real idea where I was except for a crude line on the GPS indicating the highway was somewhere a few miles ahead, but now I had a bike that could potentially grenade its gearbox if I tried to ride out. I couldn't call for help, as there was no cell reception. I couldn't expect anybody to drive up in a pickup and offer a helping hand.

I'd have to figure out my own escape, starting with the long mud puddle ahead of me.

I took all the luggage off the bike and manhandled it through the water on the left-hand side, where the muck was less deep (of course, I discovered this after getting stuck on the right-hand side). I strapped the luggage back down and after weighing my options, decided to gently ride the bike down the mountain, hoping to find help at the bottom. I figured if I lugged the bike, I'd avoid damage to the gearbox, and with the Beta's dual-sump design, I knew the oil in the engine's top end was still clean, so the valvetrain would be unaffected.

To my relief, everything held together, and after a nerve-wrack-ing ride down the mountain, I rolled out of the woods and into a backyard, where an elderly lady was tending her vegetable garden.

I must have looked a mess, because the first thing she said to me was "Do you need some help? Let me get my husband."

It turned out my new friends had a workshop in their backyard and no plans for the afternoon. My own plans for high-speed dirt riding had to go on hold as we ran a few jugs of 10W-40 through the crankcase, cleaning the water-polluted goop out.

I suspect I was the most interesting thing to pass through this area in some time, as even the neighbours popped by, with one older farmer bending down to give a hand, cursing in Gaelic as he loosened bolts. It was a reminder that the ancestors of these people had been troubled, wayfaring strangers themselves, searching for new homes after being thrown out of their own land. Their descendants still knew how to lend a hand to travellers in need.

With the bike's gearbox cleaned out, I was invited into the house for a classic Maritime dinner of beef, mashed potatoes, and canned vegetables. As a lifelong resident of Atlantic Canada, I've heard countless tourists praise our region's hospitality and generosity. After experiencing it first-hand, I've got to say, I can't think of a better place to break down.

Earlier in the day, I'd expected to make a call to the Beta distributor informing him his bike's transmission had turned into slag. But thanks to my new friends, I was headed back into the hills, well-fed, with a working motorcycle. Surely, my troubles were over.

Since it was June 21, the longest day of the year, I figured I had enough daylight left to push on and see some of the Highlands. I headed up the gravel roads of Hunter's Mountain and was looking for scenic vistas when it started to rain fast and heavy.

Earlier in the day, I'd managed to lose my rain jacket; it had either escaped its bungee and fallen trailside, or been pinched at a gas stop. Either way, I was now soaking wet, and the gas-station poncho I'd slipped under my riding jacket wasn't doing me much good. Instead of breathtaking lookouts, I was now in the early stages of hypothermia, desperately searching for shelter.

I wasn't enough of a bushcrafter to coax a fire out of the wet softwood I was travelling through, and instead of a tent, I'd brought a hammock. With a cold northerly knifing through the mountains, I knew I'd have a cold night ahead of me. Without much hope, I tried the door on the cab of an abandoned road grader, thinking it would be dry enough to get me through the night. Alas, the crew had locked it.

So, I followed the greatest travel rule of all: When all else fails, consult a map. The snowmobile map I'd found indicated another old clubhouse in my general vicinity. I figured I'd be lucky even to find the structure standing, but I pushed in that direction with minutes of daylight left, keeping an eye out for moose through the mist that was descending on the mountainside.

Moose hadn't been a major concern through the day, when visibility had been excellent, but now, in the dusk and fog, the likelihood of bumping into one was greatly increased. I pressed on, hoping local hunters were doing their part to keep the road clear. Just as the sun set, I exited the woods into a farmhouse's front yard.

An amused farmer quizzed me about who I was and where I was going while his six dogs sniffed me. He told me the snowmobile shack on my map wasn't far away—it was just below his bottom field. I fired the cycle to life, happy I hadn't had to plead with him to sleep in his horse barn to get out of the weather, and found the clubhouse in seconds.

Instead of a damp night in the woods trying to keep a fire going, I found a dry building with firewood and a pullout couch. The clubhouse hadn't been used for years, but the stale old cocoa powder in the kitchen was still palatable, and inexplicably, the power was still switched on.

It might not have been heaven, but it was a lot better than hypothermia.

The next day's riding was the best of the weekend; just as I planned, I managed to find a trail that punched through the Highlands and took me to Cheticamp, where I got on the Cabot Trail and roamed around the top of the island, flying through the corners with the sort of carefree abandon that can only be earned after a day of close calls. I returned to Friday night's snowmobile camp for another evening punctuated by the gnawing of noisy mice. Monday morning, I rode out of the woods toward Port Hawkesbury for gas and coffee.

Sitting in the service station parking lot, watching the world go by, I felt at peace with the world. People were hurrying by in every direction: vacationing in Cape Breton, hauling cars to Newfoundland, rushing for a week in Halifax. Soon I would be bucking the slipstream of traffic, vibrating wildly behind the bars of a trail bike that wasn't well-suited for highway travel, but the thought didn't bother me. I'd hit the trails, overcome a potentially disastrous mechanical problem, escaped hypothermia, and seen the Cabot Trail. I was here, now, living in the moment with a cup of coffee in my hand that tasted better than any gas-station coffee has a right to.

I didn't go to Cape Breton looking for trouble on the trail. All I wanted was smooth riding and good times. But I learned an important lesson in the rain and cold and mud: I learned that when things go wrong, you get the chance to challenge yourself and often find the problems aren't as bad as you feared.

When the road gets rough and your engine threatens to fail, you gain a better understanding of your own capabilities and limitations and the world around you. You also make new friends, because adversity brings people together.

The stones in your passway give you an appreciation for those rare occasions when everything seems to go right—and if you take the time to think about your experiences, the challenges you have faced will leave you better prepared for the inevitable days when your gears grind and the wind bites and satisfaction is still somewhere far off down the trail.

Zac Kurylyk is a writer based on Canada's east coast. His life as a father with young children doesn't allow him to explore as much of the far corners of the globe as he'd like, so he finds his adventures closer to home, usually on ill-advised motorcycle trips in bad weather. A lifelong

Maritimer, he loves nothing more than sharing his region's best back roads with visitors from around the world. He's currently working on his first book, a collection of tales of his moto misadventures.

🌐 *CanadaMotoGuide.com*
📷 *@Kawazacky*
🐦 *@Kawazacky*

FEARSOME REPUTATION

By Jeremy Kroeker

The time between realizing that you will crash your motorcycle and the actual crashing part is a real bitch. It may only be a few seconds, but you have a lot of time to think. Usually, there are questions.

"Am I really going to crash?" Yes.

"Really? There's no way to fix this?" you ask yourself, hoping for an answer from a more talented rider lurking in your subconscious. When no such rider appears, the answer is, no, you can't fix this.

Finally, acceptance. "Well, I guess this is happening," I thought. "I'm going way too fast now, and I can't make this corner." The rear wheel of my Yamaha XT 660 had locked up when I dropped a gear to scrub some speed on a steeply descending gravel road that wound its way through the mountains and sugarcane fields in Colombia.

Still in the process of my inevitable off, I wondered how I had gotten into this situation. You see, I'm 43 years old now, and I had honestly believed that my days of crashing dirt bikes were behind me. Apparently, the axiom "with age comes wisdom" doesn't apply to me yet. I'm beginning to think it may never.

Anyway, I had gotten into this mess, skidding off a corner on a mountainous road in Colombia, because I was in a hurry. I had lagged behind a group of riders in order to photograph them as they snaked along a gravel road. The road ran beside a white ribbon of water that slashed through a carpet of green, just begging to be photographed and, having done so, I was now racing to catch up. But, let's leave the crash for a moment to answer a more interesting question: why were you in Colombia in the first place?

Here we should address the elephant in the room. When I say "Colombia," several things jump to mind. At best, you'll imagine Juan Valdez standing in the coffee aisle of your local supermarket with his donkey. Of course, bringing a donkey into a supermarket is dangerous and unhygienic, but that fades to black when you imagine the greater perils of Colombia: cocaine and kidnapping.

Admit it. When you hear that someone is travelling to Colombia, most of you (who have not yet been there) recoil and ask, "Isn't that dangerous?"

That was my opinion in 2003, when I rode with my friend, Trevor, from Canada to Panama on a couple of Kawasaki KLR 650s. In fact, in my first book, *Motorcycle Therapy*, I even voiced the concern thusly:

"Trevor and I finally abandoned all hope of reaching South America. We made the decision based on time and money, but we had an unspoken understanding that our partnership could not endure the journey. We planned to explore the option of selling our bikes in Costa Rica and flying home. Failing that, we would have to drive the stupid things all the way back.

But, before getting rid of the bikes, we hoped to drive through Panama to the end of the road ... the Darien Gap. There, we'd shout, 'COLOMBIA SUCKS!' and drive away as fast as we could, giggling like schoolgirls. If all went to plan, the Colombians would never find us and we could be back in Canada before you could say 'kidnapping.'"

So, that was my thinking in 2003 and, to a degree, I was right about the perilous border region of Panama and Colombia back then. The Darien Gap has long been fraught with danger, especially for two hapless white guys speaking bad Spanish who might be mistaken for American spooks fighting the good fight against the drug trade. There and then, in that jungle, one may well disappear.

But since then, the security situation in Colombia has been steadily improving, especially since 2005. Yes, if you want to get technical, Colombia is still in a protracted civil war, but tourists will not notice. The war, as it exists now, is relegated to remote jungle regions that are almost impossible for the average person to access. In these spaces, journalists are at risk, along with police and soldiers. But, as for tourists ... if you seek danger, you may find it, but it must be your ambition.

Fearing a trip to Colombia is similar to feeling apprehension about travel to Croatia or Northern Ireland. Yes, these regions were "difficult" to visit in living memory but, when hostilities ended, or at least went underground, the media did not rampage on about how wonderful and safe these places are now. The media, in the absence of explosions and blood, just goes quiet. Of course. No news is good news, and what have you heard of Colombia lately?

This is the message the government wants to project, and that's why I was in the process of crashing a dirt bike there. I was a guest of the tourism bureau and Motolombia, one of the leading motorcycle tour and rental companies in the country. In fact, prospective guests so often ask about safety that Motolombia must deal with the concern head-on. The following customer testimonial appears in their brochure:

"IMPORTANT: Not once did I feel unsafe. In fact, Colombians are happy, helpful and engaging even though my Spanglish is marginal. – John Hubbard (USA)."

Granted, "Not once did I feel unsafe," is a modest benchmark for customer approval. If the Disneyland slogan changed from "The Happiest Place on Earth," to "You Won't Feel Unsafe," people would scratch their heads. But never mind. Other guests in the Motolombia brochure rave about the quality of the bikes, the roads, the culture, and so on, but at least one guy speaks to the fear factor.

In fact, there's an upside to Colombia's outdated, yet fearsome, reputation. It acts as a filter, keeping timid travellers at bay while open-minded explorers have free run of the country. There's a sweet spot for travel, and it's now—the years following security concerns, and before tourist hordes drive up prices and dilute authentic cultural experience. In this way, Colombia is to tourism what Egypt's Sinai Peninsula was in the 1980s, and what Iran is right now. There will be a time, maybe soon, when travellers will pine for "the way Colombia used to be," and there will be those who regret not having gone sooner.

As for me, my main regret was not having braked sooner on this twisty dirt road. Yes, I was still crashing, but I was going down fighting. After one more search of my brain for a more talented rider, a cartoon bubble of my friend Dave Coe appeared in my mind. Dave was sitting by a campfire in California, strumming a black guitar. He looked at me and said, "Brakes will never save you. But gas sometimes will." (Then my other friend, Fonzie, hijacked the bubble and, referring to pick-up strategies in bars, said, "Go ugly early.")

"Shut up, Fonzie," I thought. "That's not relevant now! Gas, you say, Dave? I'm on it!"

Now off the gravel, wide on the corner on a strip of grass that dropped sharply away into the valley, I twisted the throttle hard and turned my head in the direction of where I desperately wanted to be ... on the road. The Yamaha wore street shoes, and the drive wheel spun furiously, kicking up grass and mud, leaving a brown scimitar in the earth to mark my folly.

The bike kicked sideways, corrected, and for a moment all was good. I had avoided the big plunge and I was heading back on the road, or at least in that direction. Alas, I was still carrying way too much speed and, as the front wheel locked into a grassy rut at the edge of the road, it washed out. The knee pad on my motorcycle pants made a dimple in the dirt where it impacted, and my helmet made another hollow as it came down so close to where my tires should have been.

Whenever someone else crashes, I hasten for my camera and try to immortalize the moment and their humiliation. In this case, I let adrenaline guide me as I rushed to right the fallen machine. No photos exist.

The bike had a badly bent shift lever, and it wouldn't start. Me? I was fine. Actually, for all the drama, I probably wasn't going that fast when I finally toppled over. It's just that I'm 43, as I said earlier. These days, every crash is potentially life-altering. I've already had one hip surgery.

Anyway, I hopped into the saddle and, holding in the clutch, coasted for over a mile toward the valley bottom where I finally caught up with the group, posing for photos with friendly locals by the river.

"All good?" asked Rick, our lanky American guide who, incidentally, spoke Spanish, but with an accent similar to that of Brad Pitt's in *Inglourious Basterds*.

"Not exactly," I said, the bike still unwilling to start. "I crashed because I was racing to catch up."

"Well, that was a bad idea," said Rick, with a smile. "You're okay?" Then he dug his tool kit to fix my shift lever (another advantage to taking a guided tour: You break. Guide fixes.) The bike required no further attention—it eventually started up and ran like a champion.

I followed close behind Rick for the rest of the afternoon, never once lagging behind for photos again.

Jeremy Kroeker is the author of Motorcycle Therapy: A Canadian Adventure in Central America, *and* Through Dust and Darkness: A Motorcycle Journey of Fear and Faith in the Middle East. *With his motorcycle, he has travelled to 30 countries while managing to do at least one outrageously stupid thing in every one. He has evaded police in Egypt, tasted teargas in Israel, scrambled through minefields in Bosnia and Lebanon, and wrangled a venomous snake in Austria. One time he got a sliver in El Salvador.*

- 🌐 *MotorcycleTherapy.com*
- 🐦 *@Jeremy_Kroeker*
- 📷 *@Jeremy_Kroeker*
- 📷 *@MotorcycleTherapy*
- 📘 */OscillatorPress*
- ▶️ */JeremyKroeker*

3,000 MILES AROUND IRAN ON A TTR250

By Lois Pryce

"Iran? What d'you wanna go there for?"

This was the standard response upon announcing my plan to ride around the Islamic Republic. Once a highlight of the classic overland route to Asia, Iran had become a no-go zone for travellers in recent years, following the 2011 attack on the British embassy in Tehran. The relationship between the two nations had since sunk to an all-time low, diplomatic relations had been suspended, and the UK Foreign Office had issued hysterical travel warnings, colouring the whole of Iran in "red for danger."

It was around the time of the embassy attack that I happened to be in West London on my road-weary TTR250. I parked nearby the closed (but still heavily guarded) Iranian embassy in Kensington, and when I returned to the parking bay, I found a handwritten note on my bike. It was from a stranger, a gentleman by the name of Habib who had taken it upon himself to invite the owner of this travelling bike to visit his homeland—a plea to go and discover the "real Iran"—as opposed to the Iran of the lurid newspaper headlines that screamed about angry Islamists and rogue nuclear scientists.

Habib had addressed his note "Dear Sir," but I let him off his mistake, intrigued as to what would compel someone to make such a gesture. It wasn't so unusual to find a note on the bike. Riding

In London, you get to recognise certain motorcycles and in the small community of overland riders it is not uncommon to know someone's bike by sight, even if you don't know the owner personally. My TTR had all the identifying marks of a well-travelled machine—oversized tank, sheepskin seat, scruffy panniers, a few foreign stickers, and a general tatty appearance. But the mysterious Habib made no reference to his own motorcycle travels or ownership. I could only assume he was a regular Iranian living in London, distressed at the recent bust-up between his homeland and his adopted country—and trying out his own DIY brand of international relations.

His note got me intrigued. And he had a point. As I knew from my previous rides through the Americas and Africa, the only way to discover the reality of a country was to go out there and take a look for myself. Not with the entourage of a guided tour, or as a journalist with a suspicion-arousing press pass, but just as me—a Londoner trundling around on my bike. But Britain and Iran have a long and painful history of stormy relations, and I had no idea if I would be welcomed with open arms or chased out of the country upon arrival. After some nervous agonizing, I eventually set a departure date, applied for a visa and announced my plans to family and friends. Now I had to go.

A few months later, I was heading east, crossing the border from Turkey into Iran. Swapping my helmet for headscarf (compulsory under Iranian law) I joined the general melee that passes for a queue in Iran, anxious about what awaited me across the frontier.

The entry procedures were the usual convoluted affair and being interrogated, fingerprinted, and added to the Interpol database didn't help my paranoia. Alongside me was an elderly Iranian woman, dressed in the head-to-toe black chador, her wrinkled eyes staring and staring. I felt nervous under her gaze. This is the Iran I had feared: disapproval from a nation of hardline Islamists, suspicious of my infidel jaunt around their country on a form of transport that is outlawed for Iranian women.

Eventually, she leant in towards me with a jabbing finger.

"You, you have motor, yes?"

She repeated it again, this time accompanying it with the universal motion for riding a motorcycle: twisting the throttle, complete with engine revving noises.

"Vroom, vroom! You have motor, yes? It is you?"

There was no point in denying it; everyone had seen my bike—there was no anonymity for the lone female British motorcyclist in Iran. I had a sudden cold fear that she was an undercover member of the much-feared "Morality Police." I got a grip of my fevered imagination and 'fessed up.

"Er, yes, that's me, I have motor, yes."

She gripped my face with her big fleshy hands and gave my cheek an enthusiastic smack as a huge smile erupted across her stern features.

"Very good! Very good!" she bellowed at eardrum-piercing volume, hugging me into the voluminous folds of her chador.

She began jumping up and down, whacking me on the back and squeezing my face in her iron grip, whooping with laughter. Her motorcycle actions became more animated until she was imitating the moves of a daredevil speedway racer.

"Very good! Very good! Vroom, vroom!"

Stamped, sealed and delivered into Iran, my first challenge was the combining of Islamic clothing laws with motorcycle gear. My new look resembled the end result of a game of Picture Consequences—a confused mish-mash of vintage Belstaff jacket over a shapeless shirtdress (again, a legal requirement to hide the supposedly irresistible female form), itself worn over a pair of faded jeans tucked into battered cowboy boots. And when my open-face helmet came off, it was hastily swapped for a flowing white headscarf which only added to the bizarre get-up, resulting in something that could loosely be described as Steve McQueen meets Benazir Bhutto in Laurel Canyon circa 1972. It wasn't my finest sartorial hour.

Safely over the border, I took a breather in the northern city of Tabriz, once a major halt on the Silk Road trading route, and where Marco Polo himself had stopped on his own journey east, over 700 years earlier. In the city's huge, bustling bazaar, gold and jewels jostled for space with cheap Chinese plastic and counterfeit Western brands. In the bazaar's ancient, narrow alleys, Persian carpets were being shuttled in every direction—on shoulders, on bicycles, on the back of motorcycles. Small groups of carpet weavers sat on the ground creating their intricate patterns, fortified

with an endless supply of sweet tea. As I surveyed this exotic
scene, I realised there was not a single sign in English anywhere,
not one letter of the Roman alphabet, and not a word being spoken
that I could understand, but everywhere I went, I was welcomed
with radiant smiles—and always invited to drink tea. As I soaked
up the unfamiliar sights and scents, for a moment I forgot my TTR
parked up outside and imagined I had been transported into a
fairytale on a flying carpet.

Iranians love to eat and once I was out on the road, it became
apparent that excessive hospitality and enforced feeding was to be
a theme of my journey. Every time I stopped I was approached, and
inevitably fed, by passers-by, car drivers, and truckers who were
fascinated to see a foreign motorcycle on their roads, especially
one being ridden by a woman. Families invited me to join roadside picnics, and the men working at the toll booths were equally
welcoming. Refusing payment, they insisted on donating me their
lunch or offering me bags of peaches and pomegranates until
my panniers bulged with fruit. Everyone greeted me with great
warmth, enquiring where I was from, and most importantly, what
did I think of Iran? It soon became clear that the Iranians were
acutely aware of how their country is viewed by the rest of the
world, and suitably dismayed by this image.

The warm welcome of the Iranian people was in stark compar-
ison to the insanity that was being enacted in front of me every
minute of the day on Iran's roads. I was regularly informed that Iran
has the highest rate of road deaths in the world. This statistic was

always imparted to me with great amusement, as if it was a source of national pride. I kept reminding myself of all the hairy places I had ridden: Guatemala City, Kinshasa, Lima...

But nothing—nothing!—had prepared me for the sheer lunacy of Iranian driving. Once I'd got the hang of the fact that nobody uses indicators, lane markings are simply a waste of white paint, and that even if there are only three cars on the road, they will all drive an inch apart at the highest speed possible, I started to get into the flow.

From Tabriz, I was heading for Tehran, but before I plunged into the chaos of the capital, I took a detour into the Alborz Mountains. This range runs parallel to the coast of the Caspian Sea and includes the volcanic Mount Damavand, the highest peak in the Middle East. Here the roads emptied as I climbed thousands of feet into the wilderness, winding my way through remote peaks and jagged ravines, passing waterfalls pouring off the cliffs while eagles soared high above me. Approaching the pass, where the ancient camel caravans would have rested on their way to and from the Caspian Sea, I became stuck as the road became subsumed by deep snow. The tarmac dwindled to a slippery, rocky trail and the pass opened up before me, covered in an unexpected blanket of white. On the other side, the Caspian corniche, with its warm breeze and palm trees, came as a welcome respite.

Out of the wilderness, but back running the gauntlet on Iran's highways, I arrived in Tehran, tempted to fall to my knees and give thanks to Allah that I was still alive. Tehran is the beating heart of Iran, and it was here I truly felt I was getting under the skin of this most misunderstood country. I was introduced to a fascinating cast of characters, all with their tales of life under the regime—men and women who had been arrested by the "morality police," stories of revolution and riots, bribery and corruption, of alcohol smuggling and illicit trade in banned substances from heroin to ham.

But with a ticking visa, I couldn't hang around for too long. Iran is a vast country and it was time to hit the road once again. Its south and central regions are pure desert, dotted with a mixture of ancient, turreted towns and desolate industrial complexes protected by barbed wire, tanks, and suspicious soldiers. Out on the highways, my presence was largely accompanied by enthusiastic honking of horns and shouts of encouragement from local drivers, but the policemen I encountered took a more suspicious view of my activities. They simply couldn't comprehend the idea that I was motorcycling around their country for fun and it occurred to me that they were probably more familiar with the procedure for dealing with spies than with overland travellers. I became conscious of the need to keep a low profile—a completely impossible ambition.

Keen to escape the homicidal highways, I headed west into the Zagros Mountains, passing groups of nomadic shepherds with their flocks, making their way slowly across the hills in their traditional outfits. Then to the famous city of Isfahan with its array of fabulous mosques, minarets, palaces, and boulevards, as well as a contentious nuclear site which, I had been warned by concerned locals, must not be photographed, on pain of death. Further east and south, riding across the dry lake beds and mountains of the Dasht-e Lut desert, I found myself sweeping around great towers of red rock, crossing a landscape reminiscent of the American West. I was on my way to the ancient city of Yazd, an exotic desert settlement of domed mud-brick buildings nestling amongst a maze of narrow, winding alleyways.

In my final stop, the city of Shiraz, I found myself adopted by a retired army general and his wife. The General had lost a leg in the Iran-Iraq war of the 1980s, but he was far from a grizzled warmonger. An endlessly entertaining host, he was continually playing pranks, cracking jokes, and teaching me Farsi slang. In a moment of utterly brilliant weirdness that I could not have foreseen in my wildest imaginings, I found myself in an elevator with him, singing "The Final Countdown."

As we burst into "Da-da daa daa, da-da da da daa," I thought to myself, This is the answer to: "Iran? What d'you wanna go there for?" This is reason for travelling the world on my bike—these crazy moments of connection with people so entirely different from myself. At that moment, I was so glad I had come and discovered the real Iran.

Lois Pryce is a British travel author, journalist and broadcaster. She is also co-founder of the Adventure Travel Film Festival.

In 2003, Lois left her job at the BBC in London to ride twenty thousand miles from Alaska to the tip of South America on a small dirt bike. *Her book about this trip,* Lois on the Loose, *has been published throughout the world.*

In 2006, she rode the length of Africa, taking in the Sahara, the Congo and Angola, which resulted in her book, Red Tape and White Knuckles.

In 2013/14, intrigued by the negative image of Iran and its stormy relationship with her homeland, she made two solo motorcycle tours of the Islamic Republic—and discovered a misunderstood country full of warmth and kindness. Her latest book, Revolutionary Ride, *tells the story of these journeys.*

With her husband, adventure filmmaker Austin Vince, she is founder/curator of the Adventure Travel Film Festival, which occurs annually in the UK and Australia.

⊕ *LoisOnTheLoose.com*
🐦 *@LoisPryce*

HAZARDOUS CHOCOLATE DELIVERY

By Catherine Germillac

My back aches, and my knees are shaking. I know that squatting is a good exercise for toning leg muscles, and improving general body fitness, but I am doing no workout. At this moment there is just NO possibility for me to stand up.

Again, I hear a loud bang in a nearby street. I'd better keep hiding for now.

By the way, what is the legal tyre-tread depth in this country? Does anyone bother about it? The element of rubber I am staring at whilst squatting would be considered un-roadworthy in France. The tread on this tyre is just a souvenir of its former glory.

Another blast thunders in the distance.

This is crazy. I am literally bowing down before the tyre of a car parked in a street of Bogotá, the capital city of Colombia. I am contemplating tyre treads to keep from shaking.

For, once again, in broad daylight, I find myself caught in the middle of a gunfight.

Who is shooting at whom this time?

Why, in Colombia, is everyone shooting at each other?

At this very minute, I don't know, and I don't care.

Over the past few months, I have learned that whenever shooting erupts, it is better to hide than to ask questions.

How does a French girl end up in the middle of a Colombian street shooting?

Well, this was December 1989. A year earlier, I had left France after shipping my bike to Canada. From there, I intended to circumnavigate the world with my Yamaha 125cc within a year—no more, no less.

I got the idea to embark on this trip from a book written by an Englishman, Ted Simon. I got so taken by the stories in *Jupiter's Travels* that, once the reading was finished, I immediately registered to sit a bike test. I bought a bike shortly after that, and eventually wound up in a Colombian gunfight.

I knew nothing about the country's political turmoil when I entered Colombia. Furthermore, I spoke no Spanish upon my arrival. Nevertheless, it took me no time to grasp the dangers encountered on a daily basis by most Bogotáns.

At the point when the shots ring out, I am well behind schedule in my world-circumnavigation-in-a-year plan, with most of South America left to explore.

I find myself concentrating on the tread of the tyre located in front of me. This prevents me from shuddering so much that my precious cargo of handmade chocolate truffles spills all over the curb. For, in the hub of all this agitation, I am on a mission: I am expected to deliver two dozens of chocolate truffles to my friend Marie-Ève.

Another French national enjoying life in this part of the world, Marie-Ève is addicted to chocolate truffles, most notably mine. Made with love, and a generous quantity of strong dark Colombian chocolate, my truffles are highly regarded. So much so that I started a little business to fuel my travelling budget. I provide French expats with hand-rolled, dark-brown wonders, the kind that melt in the mouth and soothe the soul.

Obviously, the present shooting rampage I have to survive is disturbing my delivery schedule.

As I am woolgathering my attention away from the current unpleasant situation, i.e. the gun firing, I become concerned that my truffles may soften and melt. It is about time for this umpteenth gunning session to come to an end.

Just when this thought crosses my mind, silence prevails. No more shots. Not a dead body in sight. Good thing—and a nice change, if you want my opinion. After all, I have very recently escaped the bombing of the DAS (Colombia's state security headquarters) where 80 people were killed. It would be so silly to die now in a trivial interlude of street carnage.

After a few minutes of silence, people start popping their heads up. They stand up from behind cars or buildings, look around, and cautiously resume whatever activity they were doing before the gunfight began. All this is happening on the avenue where emerald deals are made on a daily basis; so it doesn't take long before discussions get animated again. In a jiffy, conversations are all about the cost of a beautiful stone or the quality of some green pebbles. Emerald is the iconic stone of Colombia and, now that the shooting is over, the *esmeralderos* are back in business!

From behind the car that has constituted my safe haven over the past fifteen minutes, I stretch and stand, too. Checking that my delicious cargo has not been damaged in the process, I resume marching through Bogotá to reach my friend's flat.

I avoid looking around me. I have no wish to see what came out of this long bullet-exchange episode. I have yet to see a dead body at close range, and I am in no hurry to do so, although there have been plenty of opportunities since my arrival in Colombia six months ago. Indeed, considering the shootings, bombings, assassinations, and other violent attacks which have succeeded one another, it is a miracle no one I know has yet been caught in a cross-fire. When one hears about the bloodshed taking place all over the country, one cannot avoid wondering when and where a stray bullet could find its way to one's skull. After all, no matter what one might think, it does not only happen to others.

At the very beginning of my stay in Colombia, most violent actions occurring in Bogotá were directed at buildings, at night. The damages were limited to glass projections and partly derelict edifices. Two friends of mine had even found a nickname for the group of people responsible for these actions: *el cartel de los vidrieros* or "the glaziers' cartel."

Here, it must be noted that those two buddies had recently opened their own window repair shop. In a tiny six-square-metre stall, they accumulated large glass sheets and mirror plates. Upon request, they could measure and cut a new window pane, or a mirror to install in a pretty damsel's bedroom or a boutique. And there was definitely no lack of business opportunities at the time!

On one occasion, I was returning home after a late dinner in town with one of these gentlemen glaziers, Juan-Carlos, when a bomb exploded in a street we had just come through. Immediately, and apparently not as affected by the situation as I was, he told me to accompany him to the location of the blast. "There is business to be done, come and help me," he said.

Luckily, nobody was hurt; there were only material damages to report.

Amidst glass debris, and before fearful, bleary-eyed inhabitants, Juan-Carlos swiftly advertised his wares and services for window replacement. His cunning plan: deliver pristine windowpanes the following morning, even if that meant working all through the night.

Climbing up the stairs of the most affected buildings, he knocked on doors, offering his services. Meanwhile, I stood in the street, still somewhat in a daze, armed with just a notepad and a pen. Leaning over the busted window frames, he shouted measurements, which I hastily scribbled on the notepad, along with names and flat numbers. It went on like that for a couple of hours.

Back near my place, located not far from his shop, he went to wake up his business partner, who also happened to be one of his cousins. Both of them worked until dawn, cutting glass, wrapping it, and assembling orders ready for delivery.

Several days later, due to an avalanche of orders, they even hired me. They taught me how to cut glass and make windowpanes. That is how I found myself learning a new trade: window-maker.

Yes, in those days, it seemed that bombing was good for business; at least for some individuals.

The resilience of Colombian people in time of adversity has never ceased to amaze me. Those I met were tough cookies; courageous and hardworking, a far cry from the bunch of drug dealers or mules often portrayed when one mentions the word *colombiano*. Even when the attacks meant death, locals' reaction was more often than not "Let's go out and party."

Along with friends and perfect strangers, I sometimes found myself toasting life with *aguardiente*—a popular aniseed-based alcohol beverage—in a low-life Bogotá drinking hole after some disgraceful bombing attack. In my view, there was nothing reprehensible in doing so. It was just a natural and reassuring approach to the fragility of life; life which could disappear within seconds in the hands of some invisible evil people.

Colombians knew it too well. Their response resumed to a big "F***-off" attitude—paired up with salsa music, laughter, and drinks.

I am mentally reviewing all these worrisome situations in Colombia when I finally reach my friend's flat, still carrying my bundle of chocolate. I shall never forget the look on her face when she opens her door. I guess that is the look people have when they see a ghost: a mix of total disbelief, absolute shock, tinted with a touch of panic ... or is it fear? Her grey-green eyes open wide, but no sound comes out of her mouth. A fish taken away from its tank could not look more surprised. After the image comes the sound, at last:

"What the hell are you doing here? And how did you get here? Did you come on your own? Don't you know what's going on in town? Are you mad to have gone out in the streets with what's going on right now? Are you all right?"

When I lift my precious cargo, waving it in front of her eyes, the ongoing flow of questions changes to astounded comments:

"I don't believe it! You brought your truffles! You could have waited until tomorrow! You are crazy! You shouldn't have ventured outside when you heard the shooting! You could have been shot!"

As soon as my friend is reassured about my physical health— since she gives up enquiring about my mental health—she insists on hosting me for the night. She argues it will be too dangerous for me to risk the streets again.

At this time, I can hear no more shooting coming from the streets. The muffled noise of traffic acts like a reassuring sound, a perfect indicator that life is back to normal in this unpredictable city.

That night, after indulging in far too many truffles shared with my friend, I lie down on the sofa. In my mind, I revisit the places where I have been offered shelter, and the faces of those hosts, good enough to invite me into their homes when I needed it most.

I realise how lucky I have been ever since I set foot in Colombia. I have been blessed with the people who crossed my path, despite hazardous circumstances I have sometimes encountered. This applies to my entire journey since I landed in Canada.

Before I fall asleep, once again a broad smile finds its way to my lips. Somehow, I sense there will be more shelters and more friendly faces to come my way.

*

A year later, I embarked on yet another chocolate truffle delivery. This time it took place in Ecuador. What did it mean? No more street shootings, and above all, no need to hide behind cars, waiting for bullets to stop flying past my head.

In Quito, I proudly entered the French embassy, carrying an order of 12 dozen chocolate truffles carefully bundled in brightly coloured wrapping paper. The scent of cocoa powder fluttered to my nostrils, carrying away the memory of the smell of gunpowder that nearly spoiled a previous delivery.

A French citizen, Catherine Germillac has travelled extensively with her Yamaha 125 DTMX, her first and only bike to this day, named Désirée. When the wanderlust bug caught her, Catherine shipped her bike to Canada, embarking solo on what unexpectedly became a six-year journey.

From Montreal, she started her globe-trotting adventure before reaching Ushuaia ... five years later.

In Valparaiso, Chile, she shipped her beloved motorcycle to Australia, where she wandered for another year.

Back in Europe, she spent several years in Scotland before returning to Brittany, France, where she currently lives.

She still enjoys riding around Europe at the crazy pace of 80 kilometres per hour.

30 years on, Désirée is still alive and well. Thank you for asking.

CHANGE FOR A BRIBE?

By Allan Karl

Staying just one day past a visa deadline can get a traveller in trouble. Yet I push my stay in Mexico a few days too long. I might be detained, fined, or worse. I've always found, however, that a traveller's best weapon against any potential problem or threat is a bright smile.

Worried that the border guards will notice as I walk to the border control office, I dismount my bike and flash my best smile.

This time, my secret weapon works. A rhythmic pounding of three rubber stamps later, my wrinkled and torn customs document is approved. The gun-toting guards lift the gate and let me cross into Guatemala.

As I mount my bike, I am a little apprehensive. Warnings of corrupt Latin American cops are splattered across dozens of travel blogs, forums, and Facebook groups. So, months before crossing the border into Latin America, I make a deal with myself: never bribe, always negotiate.

For months I have travelled the back roads of Central and South America. So far, the armed, uniformed, and hyper-fast-Spanish-speaking officers at police and military checkpoints have been unsuccessful in their attempts to extort a bribe from me.

My command of the Spanish language improves with every conversation, and so I begin to think I can talk my way out of most anything.

The weather, like the cops, can also be threatening. Riding through the tropics is hot any time of the year. If the blistering heat doesn't turn a motorcycle riding suit into a sauna, then the pounding rain will sideline a rider for hours—even days.

As I wind my way through narrow, twisting turns, through palm and banana plantations, and then across single-lane wooden bridges shared with railroad tracks, the sun blazes down. I am baking in my suit. The slight breeze filtering through the vents in my riding jacket is refreshing, but barely keeps me cool. I must maintain speed to keep the breeze flowing.

But when I ride up to a line of slow-moving vehicles, I'm forced to slow down. The temperature inside my suit soars.

"What's the holdup?" I wonder. Beyond the curve, I see an ancient, miniature Renault station wagon. It hobbles along at barely 20 miles an hour. There are four people crammed into the front seat and another five or six in the back. Several chickens strapped to the roof are barely balanced among a teetering tower of feeble wooden crates. Not only is the wagon overloaded, the rear wheels are two different sizes. One by one, the cars ahead of me pass the Renault, the turtle in this creeping parade. Then it's my turn.

As the hare accelerates and passes the turtle, the breeze—at last—cools me.

I am startled by staccato honking from something zooming up behind me. In my side mirror I notice a police officer. He is riding an old 600cc Yamaha motorcycle. Its vintage red bubble-gum lamp, atop a three-foot high stanchion, is spinning. He's in a hurry.

He zooms up next to my bike and points at me. I smile and nod. Then I do what all motorcyclists do when crossing paths with another rider: I turn to him, nod, and wave back.

I turn my gaze to the road ahead and continue to ride.

He feverishly honks once more, then motions with his hand again.

I honk back, smile, nod, and wave.

More honking.

Through the dirty face-shield of his badly scuffed helmet, I see his frustration. He honks three more times and, with determined and purposeful animation, points to the side of the road.

Uh-oh. I pull over.

He barely looks at my passport, international driver's license, and motorcycle import papers before stuffing them inside and hoisting up the pocket zipper of his jacket. He points to the bags on my bike and then to his eyes. He wants to look.

I unlock my bags and he pokes around.

When I address him formally in Spanish, he starts talking faster. I know what he's saying, but don't give in. Instead, I just shrug. "Como?" (Huh?)

"Linea doble! Linea doble! No cruce la linea doble!" (Don't cross the double line.)

I shrug.

He pulls a small notepad from his back pocket and scribbles a sketch of a two-lane road with two lines down the middle. He then draws a line crossing those two lines and back. "Linea doble! No cruce!"

Okay. He got me. I did cross the double line. Did he just happen to see me? Or did he have a temporary memory lapse? What about the six cars that crossed that line just seconds before I did?

He pulls out another notepad, this one complete with loose sheets of carbon paper. He fits one of the carbons between two pages. He looks at me, waiting.

I say nothing, and smile.

He taps the point of his pen on the pad and glares coldly at me.

It's clear he wants me to offer money, a bribe. I stay silent. He shoves the notepad back into his pocket.

"Vamos a la estación de policia." (We're going to the police station.)

At this point many travellers might give in. But I've got another secret weapon.

What he doesn't realize is that at this moment I have what most tourists and travellers don't: time. I can think of nothing more exciting and interesting than to visit and experience a Central American police station.

"Vamos, okay, vamos," I agree.

This is not the answer he expected or wanted. He's frustrated again.

Then, in another lapse-of-memory moment, the police officer makes a startling statement.

"No, olvidé," he says (I forgot), pulling the pad out of his pocket again.

He suddenly remembers the police station is closed for three days. He explains that he must hold my documents until then.

I don't believe him, but realize I'm beat. I must buy my way out of here. It's true, I did break the law.

It occurs to me that I have only one bill in my pocket. It's the equivalent of about twenty dollars, a lot of money to him. I know he would let me go for as few as five dollars. I could bluff and tell him I only have credit cards, no cash. But that would be pushing my luck. I need those documents. Yet, there's no way I want to give him my last twenty.

I thrust my hand into my pocket, feel the bill as I crumple it in my palm. I think fast, and as I pull out the bill, I blurt in Spanish that my wallet was stolen.

I explain that this twenty is the only cash I have until I can get to a city.

"Necessito comprar petrol," I plead with him that I need to buy fuel.

I flash the twenty. "Tienes cambio?" I ask him if he has change.

I know he would accept less than half of my twenty dollars, but there is a big bill in the palm of my hand—and he has a gringo in his.

He simply shrugs. He says he's got no money, no change.

We are at both ends of our respective ropes. I ask if I can go, appealing to his humanity, or so I hope. When he is just about to give in, say yes, I sense he has another idea.

He walks over to my bike and grabs the two spare 1.5L fuel bottles he saw when inspecting my bags. He carries them to his police bike. He then disconnects his fuel line and fills both of my spare fuel bottles.

Proudly, he tightens the caps and hands them to me. "Hay petrol!" (Here's your gas.)

What can I do? I hand him my only bill and continue my journey south. He beat me.

This was the first, and last, time I ever bribed a police officer during my three-year journey. It's likely he is, perhaps, the only officer in Latin America to offer fuel as change for a bribe.

The turtle beat me, too.

Allan Karl, also known as WorldRider, is the bestselling author of FORKS: Three Years. Five Continents. One Motorcycle. A Quest for Culture, Cuisine, *and Connection, a book that chronicles his three-year solo motorcycle journey around the world through stories, photographs, food, and recipes. He is also host of* Food Explorer, *a television series on the Cooking Channel about Allan's quest to discover unique cultures and interesting food. Allan has travelled to more than 75 countries and is on a mission to travel overland to every country in the world. He is a professional speaker, motorcycle adventurer, award-winning photographer, and television host. He lives in Leucadia, California, but rides and travels all over the world.*

- 🌐 *AllanKarl.com*
- 📄 *WorldRider.com/blog*
- 🐦 *@WorldRider*
- 📷 *@WorldRider*
- 📘 */worldrider.pro*

LOSING MY IDENTITY

By Paddy Tyson

My head was forced forward awkwardly, my chin pressing into my chest. The side of my face almost touched the wooden shelf before me. I was soaked in sweat, but powerful hands continued to simultaneously grip and pummel me. I couldn't quite glimpse in the mirror above who it was that had control of me now, but straining my eyes to the left, I was able to see through the doorway, past the tattered curtain, to the hot, dusty street beyond. Somewhere out there I could hear a radio, but with the sun so high in the sky and the temperature incredible, few would be venturing far from the shade. But just now I wished to. The only other sounds ricocheting around this wooden shack came from my joints, as my limbs were forced into positions unimaginable. This was not what I'd planned at all.

I was pulled back in the chair—two of them had me now—and as I twisted around to face my tormentors, I noticed a new darkness outside, and there was a momentary lull in proceedings. I looked again towards the street. It was an elephant, the only real traffic I'd seen all day.

Sauraha village nestles on the banks of the East Rapti River in southern Nepal. Right on the edge of the Chitwan National Park, it is a draw for tourists and those who make a living from them, one way or another. However, Nepal is not a wealthy country, and this is not a wealthy place within it. The traffic for much of the morning had been single track, or elephantine, but as always, everyone had been friendly.

"Namaste!" The barber had called out the greeting as I wandered too close to the shack an hour earlier. A wet shave, I thought, that's something I've never experienced. What better place to let a man attack me with a cut-throat razor that could already have grazed a hundred jugulars? It mattered little that we didn't share a common tongue—I just prayed that I'd keep mine. But somehow that lack of communication had led me here, to this: experiencing a full-body massage and surreally watching an elephant lumber past, distorted through the lens of sweat flowing ceaselessly from my brow. And yet a huge part of me relished the complete lack of control.

I'd submitted absolutely to whatever my fate would be, in a manner not dissimilar to that of the local drivers. That's what happens in Nepal. It's a country that gets under your skin and where you relinquish a huge part of what you may feel to be important. And it can happen quickly. Yes, I'd been here before, but I was now only eight days' riding out of Kathmandu and already a million miles from the stresses of life in the UK. I'd already experienced so many uniquely Nepali experiences and been immersed in so much of what the country had to offer; why shouldn't the only traffic be elephants? And why shouldn't these men be contorting my limbs?

I'd slept in homestays and been blessed in the mornings. I'd used my plodding Enfield to assault tracks that many feel should only be tackled on light dirt bikes, and spent time talking to

Coke-drinking sadhus. I'd woken in the tiny hill village of Dhampus at five o'clock to watch the sun rise and illuminate the snow-clad slopes of the stunning Annapurna ranges, and later enjoyed ice-cold bottles of refreshing Everest beer beneath thatched roofs and in front of mind-blowing vistas. I had picked up a few helmetless hitch-hikers and enjoyed easy and enlightening conversations as I'd ridden the country's byways. I'd happened upon festivals of various theological persuasions and dodged thousands of Nepal's erratically ridden Hero-Honda Splendor 100s. As I always do in Nepal, I felt I was finding my real identity.

And then I nearly lost it.

Just a couple of days before reaching Chitwan National Park, I'd been enjoying the mountains for the vistas, curves, and cooler air they provide, and was riding the Siddhartha Highway, one of the four main north-south thoroughfares in Nepal. It's right up there in my top ten of the world's most incredible riding roads. Running 180 kilometres southward from the mighty Annapurna Ranges in the Himalaya to the hot plains that border India, the Siddhartha doesn't purport to be anything like the highest motorable road, but it is perhaps one of the world's twistiest. This discourages freight and makes it an absolute delight for motorcyclists. It climbs south-wards from the lakeside at Pokhara, Nepal's second city, and then hugs the sides of the Adhi Khola valley, providing view after view for which there are insufficient superlatives.

In this instance, my mirrors remained full of the pesky Hero-Honda tailing me, its rider's stoical expression unchanging as his bare feet snicked another gear and his shirt fluttered in the breeze. Corner after corner after corner, the Enfield 500 EFI beneath me demonstrated just how adept it was at climbing mountains, the simple single thumping away without complaint, pulling strongly up every new incline. If I threw caution to the wind and ignored the very real chance that the tarmac could end mid-bend, or free-range children would be tending sacred cattle on the next apex, it was even possible to gently scrub the footpegs or the long, slender exhaust. But the little Honda was always there, somewhere in my rear view. In his favour, he was a rider alone, unencumbered by the usual Sherpa cargo of five family members, but his persistence really was admirable—if a little annoying and challenging to my misplaced sense of masculinity.

When the topography and civil engineers provided available width between the cliffs and the void, I pulled over just to stop and take it all in. The little black Honda arrived a little after. Its rider dismounted and approached. Like a true Westerner, I prepared for confrontation. Calmly and respectfully, like all Nepalis, Shree Raj Baral, a local physics teacher, explained that I had dropped my passport and accompanying documentation some 15 kilometres earlier. The villagers who'd noticed my identity lying on the road had assigned him the task of giving chase. Shree's attitude, the fantastic road we were enjoying, and the landscape we stood within encapsulated the Nepalese experience.

Who can be angry in this place? The driving is dreadful, but none of it is malicious. Drivers smile and wave genuinely, as they leave you nowhere to go on a mountain track, or as they turn across your path in downtown Kathmandu. It's a relaxed chaos, one of noise and filth and fun. And endemic corruption. I passed queues of stationary bikes, hundreds of metres long and five or six bikes deep, cordoned off by the military. Even Splendor 100s need fuel and there's precious little of that available, so much of the day can be spent waiting, with pleasant, resigned acceptance. If Nepal doesn't pay its bills, why should India supply the oil? And when it does, if the tanker drivers haven't been paid, why shouldn't they stop off and make a few deliveries for cash between border and city? It's fate. Chill.

After negotiating the dusty tracks in the mountains to the south of the city, I dived into the cut and thrust of central Kathmandu; down back streets and past the aromatic open sewer known as the Bagmati River. The mighty Enfield thundered down alleyways and along what appeared to be pathways, bisecting the major thorough-fares where only two-wheeled vehicles move with any aplomb. A crazy run through a crazy city—exhilarating, exhausting—to meet the exceptional Lily, a French-American-English expat who has dedicated herself to the assistance of others.

Lily has embraced this colourful country and given herself to orphan girls of Nepal who have fallen foul of poverty, abuse, or internal displacement. She parents and educates but doesn't preach or dictate, equipping girls from seven to 17 with life skills... and shelter while they accrue them. She can't do everything, but she tries, and to pay the bills she's every bit as inventive as courageous. A previous contributor to *Overland* Magazine, I had to meet her, offering assistance in some small way. It seems as nothing, but at least a water supply might ensure the smiles stay on those happy faces.

Nepal remains a predominantly pedestrian nation. The nature of the mighty mountain ranges means that the few major highways are consigned to a handful of valley floors and the rest of the infrastructure remains wanting. Wanting for everything, really, not least for the annual monsoons to stop destroying whatever tracks and bridges have been created in the hinterlands.

But it's all heaven for bikes. Nearly 90% of Nepal's registered vehicles are motorcycles; the nation couldn't survive without them. They manage any terrain in any weather and easily seat six. But as we returned across the capital to our hotel in the Thamel district, dodging kamikaze riders and doing my best to adopt the local style: studiously ignoring roundabouts or any highway code, I passed a rider at the side of the street, remonstrating with two policemen who had pulled him over. For the life of me I can't conceive of the traffic offence he must have committed to deserve such treatment. It will remain forever a mystery and something I'll ponder next time I'm watching elephants amble past as I'm being pummelled in a shack.

Paddy Tyson is a wandering Irishman who has been travelling the world by motorcycle since 1991. He writes for various motorcycle publications in the UK and North America and provides light-hearted entertainment for those willing to sit through a presentation of earlier travels. Previously a lecturer, journalist, political campaigner and dispatch rider, he now edits Overland *and is an advisor for The Ted Simon Foundation and a director of Shuvvy Press Ltd. He drinks an inordinate amount of tea. Paddy is the author of* The Hunt for Puerto Del Faglioli: A Motorcycle Adventure in Search of the Improbable.

🌐 *PaddyTyson.com*
🌐 *OverlandMag.com*

DEATH AND BEAUTY ON THE ROAD TO KANYAKUMARI

By Carla King

I walk into the water at the pointy tip end of India to feel the Trinity ebb and flow around my ankles. Here is the confluence of the Arabian Sea, the Indian Ocean and the Bengal Sea. Here are the pilgrims, gazing out to sea, splashing in the shallows, and settling on the sand to contemplate and to pray to this great trinity—the creator, the protector, the destroyer. Brahma, Vishnu, Shiva.

The father, the son, the holy ghost.

I chose to ride an obscure little back road from Madurai to Kanyakumari, to the end of India. It was a mistake. It is often a mistake to choose a back road in a country where even the main roads are like back roads. It began well enough, lush and tropical, but changed abruptly to scrub and desolation. Some time recently, asphalt had been poured thinly onto the dry, golden earth, resulting in a winding black ribbon that was already crumbling at the edges into dust.

The motorcycle chugged along undisturbed, but for me it was a lonely road, like the road to Big Bend through a dry Texas valley toward the Rio Grande; like the road through the Gobi Desert with its windswept snakes of sand wending south to the Yellow River. It's along these roads that you start wondering if, by some fluke, you are the last living person in the world, and then suddenly someone appears, walking from somewhere to nowhere.

Where is she going, that woman in a bright green sari carrying the huge bundle of twigs on her head? And those two men with newly carved wooden pitchforks slung over their shoulders—where might they use them, less than a day's walk away?

Another hour goes by and I'm still wondering where those people came from, where they were going. In four hours, I stopped three times for other vehicles—two buses and a truck that kindly didn't force me off into the ditch. I stopped once for a herd of cows and once for a black spotted goat that trotted back and forth on the asphalt in panic. I might have dreamt my last forced halt, which was to let dozens of miniature burros pass by. They swarmed around the motorcycle, their long ears brushing my mirrors as they trotted toward an oasis with one tiny pond and a few spindly coconut trees. The scent of hot fur and manure lingered a moment, and then there was only dry heat in a landscape of sand and aloe and acacia and twisted little trees with flat tops, with a few withered leaves clinging to dry branches.

Still no village, still no petrol station—the source of a helpless underlying worry that remains with me. I follow the sun, setting its glare in my right eye, and continue down this southwest back road, as if I had a choice. I am twenty kilometres into the reserve tank, and my worry grows, but just when the engine begins to stutter, civilization appears.

I coast to the pump and welcome the shimmering rise of petrol fumes as the attendant splashes the first precious drops into the tank. I stand waiting for the tank to fill as touts swarm me with promises of cheap hotels but escape toward the sea to join the pilgrims. Busloads of pilgrims.

Finding a place among them on the beach, I watch the horizon from this spot at the end of the world, the end of their world.

The women are draped in all colours of silks and cottons, scarves over their heads and gold discs in their nostrils, bangles on their wrists and ankles and barefoot, barefoot for all of their lives. A man in white and orange is having his photo taken to commemorate the moment, the highlight of his pilgrimage. He adjusts his white turban and strikes a severe pose, knee-deep in the sea. Beyond him a few people splash in the water, protected by a reef of smooth brown rocks that breaks the waves.

A sun-blackened hippie wrapped in gauzy Indian cotton perches on a larger rock, picking out a tune on an exotic small guitar. He smiles at me, then picks up the rhythm as two women wade into the water up to their thighs, their saris floating in the gently heaving tide like yellow and lavender seaweed. I press my bare feet into the sand and walk in after them, the brown cotton of my pants darkening with water.

The sea is warm and the salt stings my wounds. The sun is falling. The faces around me are quiet and smooth in meditation. Many, sitting in groups on the sand, close their eyes.

The bald heads of those who gave their hair at Tirupati are smeared with yellow ash. Nearly every forehead is dotted with red kumkum powder, swiped on by the priest during today's darshan blessing at the temple. They know why they are here, these pilgrims. They come in ragtag groups and huddle together around the buses in which they arrive. They make a tiny space for living, cooking, and sleeping. They defecate onto the rocks at the sea wall at dawn and dusk. They visit the temple, worship, and then gather again, kneading dough for chapattis, flattening them into discs, tossing them into a fire. Someone stirs a huge pot of watery yellow dahl.

They experience hardship, as is appropriate on a pilgrimage. The word "sacred" has its roots in the word "sacrifice," and they know the meaning of both. Their journey here was long and difficult and wasted their savings. They are poor, but they, at least, know what they are looking for. They, at least, know what they have found: the fulfillment of an agreement made from the beginnings of one of their many lives. They know that this life is only one of many more to come.

I say that I am not a seeker, yet here I am in a country where seeking and finding is a natural part of life. Road signs warn, "Be Careful, Only One Life," but to Hindus, karma is a factor that tempers the fear of the end of this life, and if you die because you are driving like a maniac, well, it's out of your hands. It's your karma. But no matter, previous lives well lived promise reward in the next. You can speed up the process toward enlightenment by walking around mountains and making offerings to deities and performing countless other rituals. Such rituals! They are lovely and frightful.

I copied the movements, the outward signs of worship, wanting to feel what these pilgrims feel. I followed carefully in the bare footsteps of those walking through darkened hallways, down the stairs to the inner sanctum. I performed the puja ceremony to the temple gods along with the others, and received my darshan from the priest. My tender feet have been burned on hot stones and sliced on broken coconut shells. I am not tough enough. But I am here now. Now I stand in the sea, my forehead swiped with red kumkum powder. Paying respects. Trying to understand.

I am a child-person here, a foreigner, and they forgive me. Religion is not a game or entertainment for tourists, and I am a tourist, an unintentional spiritual tourist in this land of temples and sacred mountains. I have always made a little bit of fun of seekers, but India does something to you that creates a wondering. Within a week of my arrival, I found myself at the Aurobindo ashram, and the next day I was meditating with the largest crystal in the world. There I found an energy that removed me from my physical self for just a little less than an hour. I floated for days on that energy, and I know that whatever shaped that clear, pure stone is a spiritual force to be taken seriously, as serious as the velocity at which I hit the ground seven days ago.

I killed a dog. Does that shave time from my process of enlightenment? I rub the seawater into my wounds and the salt sting is good. The thick scabs that have formed on the tops of my wrists, my knees, and my left shoulder are softening and beginning to bleed again. I remember the speedometer reading forty miles per hour and the improbable impact, then the tumbling, the sound of my helmet bouncing in my ears, and then blessed landing, unconsciousness, then choking on water being poured on my face.

The dog was still screaming as they took my keys and put me in the van. They were Christian missionaries, Indians in fluttering white saris. They put me in the back, and I looked out the window. The dog lay still at the side of the road. It was a gray-black dog, an adult, healthy and vibrant, with short, shiny fur. There was no blood, but it lay panting heavily, its eyes open wide. I know I hit it square on, right in the middle. The moment before I hit it is frozen in my memory.

"Is the dog dead?" I asked the woman in the green sari who was performing Hindu blessings over my bloody knee. "No," she said. "It is not yet dead." One of the missionaries started the motorcycle. Miraculously, it was undamaged.

"It will be dead soon?" I asked. "Yes," she said. "It will soon be dead." She said one last prayer, and left me to the missionaries.

No one did anything about the dog. I hated it for crossing the road like that, without looking. I thought it deserved to die, the stupid, hateful creature. And then I was sorry. So sorry. Weeks later, I still fluctuate between the hate and the sorrow, and I remember, along with this confusion, the feeling of the blood, so warm at my knee, and then colder as it ran down my leg, soaking the white fabric of the fine cotton saris folded under me. At the time I didn't even wonder at the fate of my knee, or of the rest of my trip. I was enfolded and unravelled, leaving my fate in hands other than my own. In India you look around and realize that since you've arrived there is no moment—not even one—when you can escape knowing where you are.

Now the sun sinks into the sea and I become a pilgrim. I am still here, in India, with all its dirt and beauty. Each is balanced by the other; there is nothing between. There is the boy with the twisted legs and the wide black eyes skittering on his hands along the sidewalk, silently begging. The woman, piebald with leprosy, glaring hate and spirit. The crone with her hand sticking from a ragged silk sari, her toothless mouth croaking "maw, maw."

There is the glossy white cow chewing banana peels and pomegranate husks. The girl child supporting her baby sister on a tiny, jutted hip. A line of sadhus in orange robes, sitting with their beards and their hollowed-out gourds along the swept-clean gates of an ashram. A stoned hippie arguing with a rickshaw driver over a nickel's worth of taxi fare. Goats tossing their heads to rip through plastic bags at garbage piles, yellow eyes glittering under the streetlight. An aluminum vat of green chili peppers popping and sizzling. Discarded banana leaves slimy with yellow curry lying next to a pile of shit by the rickshaw-pullers' curb. It is difficult to look but I feel that if I stay quiet enough for long enough and do what they do, my gaze may glimpse the glimmer of the nowhere that is the beauty.

Carla King's motorcycle misadventures began at age 14 in rural North Carolina, when she identified the broken-down Honda Enduro in the barn as her escape vehicle. Her dad told her, "If you can fix it, you can ride it," unaware that he was setting her up for a career in adventure travel. She started with day-long jaunts through tobacco fields and creeks and—when the family moved to California—the coast and the mountains throughout the state. A six-week solo journey through France in the '80s led to months-long sojourns in Europe, China, Africa and India. In the mid-'90s, Carla combined her love of travel, technology, mechanics, writing, and publishing to create the first real-time online travelogue (now called blogs), and began publishing her work and helping others self-publish.

⊕ *CarlaKing.com*
🐦 *@MissAdventuring*

RIDING HIGH

By Ted Simon

The following story is an excerpt from the book
Riding High, *published by Jupitalia Productions. It*
has been edited for length. Used with permission.

Having left London in 1973 with my motorcycle, I arrived on the
island of Penang in Malaysia nearly two years later, expecting to
continue on into Thailand. I was even hoping that I might find a
way to get through or around Burma on my way to India, but an
accident to my eye landed me in hospital, and by the time I had
recovered there was no longer time. I had booked a passage on the
Chidambaram to Madras and I could manage only a short journey
into Thailand.

The journey I had set myself that first day out of Penang could
not have been simpler. From the border to Haad Yai was only
thirty miles or so on a good flat road. There was no need to change
money. American dollars were acceptable everywhere at a generally agreed rate of 20 baht to the dollar. In any case there was
nothing I needed to buy before I arrived.

I tried to settle down on the bike and recover my old easy
rhythm, but it would not come. Some of this I could put down
to the nature of the excursion itself. It felt strange and somehow

offensive to be making a circular tour limited to a few days and to know that I would be coming back on this same road. I could not hope to see more than a small southern patch of the country and the thought was depressing. Compared with the grand, sweeping journeys I was accustomed to making across countries and continents, it seemed like a mean little trip.

I knew it was foolish thinking. It meant that I had lost touch with the real excitement of travel, which is a thing of each day, each hour, each moment. Instead I was trying to rebuild my confidence on an abstract image of myself as the great circumnavigator, forever pressing on into the unknown. Realizing this, and without T'an to feed me my daily dose of flattery, my morale slumped even further.

It was a vicious circle. To be worth making at all a journey has to be made in the mind as much as in the world of objects and dimensions. What value can there be in seeing or experiencing anything for the first time unless it comes as a revelation? And for that to happen, some previously held thought or belief must be confounded, or enhanced, or even transcended. What difference can it make otherwise to see a redwood tree, a tiger, or a humming bird?

Happily it is beyond the capacity of human beings to anticipate things exactly. How one would laugh at someone who, shown an elephant for the first time, said "Ah, yes, just as I expected." But there certainly are people for whom the first experience of an elephant would be no special event.

Everything depends on the elephant in the mind and the amount of imaginative effort that has been lavished on it. If it is a mere sketch or outline, then as long as the real thing roughly resembles it, that will do. There is no reason, after all, for being more fascinated by real elephants than by imaginary ones. If, on the other hand, you have spent years doting on the idea of elephants; if you have fired your imagination to divine what it must be like to touch its hide, to feel its breath, to hear it snorting and trumpeting, to climb up like Sabu and ride in majesty on its back, then the real experience when it comes is a source of lasting wonder and interest.

An army may march on its stomach, driven by orders, but a traveler must fly on the wings of imagination, like Quixote, fuelled by the fantasies of a lifetime. What I suffered, as I came into Thailand, was a collapse of the imagination. I went along staring about me in dull discomfort, hoping that something would happen soon to get me flying again.

I had heard nothing about Haad Yai to recommend it except as a stopping place on the way. As I rode through it I saw only shops, houses, and small businesses. King's Hotel caught my eye first, with its expensive modern facade proclaiming that it would cost too much for me. Then, next door, squatting in the shadow of its neighbour, I noticed a small restaurant with a dingy hotel sign added as an afterthought.

I parked the bike outside the door where I would be able to see it, stuffed my keys and gloves into my helmet, and looked inside the restaurant. It was a grubby fly-blown place and I would have left to try elsewhere if a voice had not called out to me.

"Hello. Come and sit down."

The invitation came from a tall, thin European with lank blond hair who was twisted around in his chair to see me. Opposite him sat another man, shorter, heavier, with a carefully trimmed black beard, who stared at me with a stony expression. I sat next to the darker man to keep my eye on the bike. There were two smeared Coca-Cola bottles between them.

"Are you staying here?" I asked. They said they were, and that it was cheap. The blond man with an obviously Scandinavian accent said he was Norwegian. His companion was Swiss. We exchanged the usual details, where we were going, where we had come from. They had both just arrived from Bangkok. The Norwegian had no particular plans except, he said, "to look for a girl." He appeared gloomy and quite nervous, and talked about getting a girl as someone who, feeling the flu coming on, might talk of getting some aspirin.

The Swiss was going on to Malaysia, and was full of complaints about the arrogance and deceitfulness of the Thais. He had been cheated and his camera had been stolen.

"Everyone here loses his camera," he said, bitterly. "You must watch your stuff like an eagle. The Americans have spoiled this country completely. It is all corrupted. One time it was not like this. There was another tradition. Wherever you went, people were always giving freely what they had. Now they are just taking all they can."

"You are quite right..." said the Norwegian. He spoke an efficient but mechanical English which he drove out of his mouth in lurches of fluency, like a tank turning a corner.

"You are quite right"—grind—"Thailand was full of Americans"—judder—"the people were dependent on them"—clank—"now they are gone..."

His theory was that the Thais had become greedy and obstreperous because the Americans, having spent freely during the Viet Nam war, had now abandoned them in the grip of a habit they could not afford.

The Swiss listened with an air of disapproval, which seemed habitual. A man came through from a door behind the counter and I asked him for a room. He took me up to the first floor. It had been divided into boxes with flimsy hardboard partitions, and for 35 baht I got one of these with two narrow beds, a fan, and a gauze-covered hatch escaping onto the narrow space between the hotels. I took all my things off the bike and humped them up the wooden stairs, locking them into my cubicle with the padlock provided. The management consented to bring the bike into the restaurant at night when they locked up.

It was still only mid-afternoon. I went back to my seat downstairs and was wondering what to do when two Thais came in from the street, smiling softly in an ingratiating but businesslike way.

One, with a wispy black moustache and wearing an American sport coat, said:

"We are ready now. You can come along, please."

The Norwegian turned his blanched blue eyes on me.

"We are going to some houses to see the girls. You should come too. Maybe you can find one you like."

"Sure, mister," said the Thai. "You come for the ride."

I overcame my distaste and agreed to go "for the ride." We walked outside and climbed into the back of a miniature Japanese bus. There were two short wooden benches, with room perhaps for a party of six or eight. I wondered whether we were going to pick up other passengers for the tour. It seemed like a peculiar way to proceed to the temples of Eros. I had always imagined that one would be slightly drunk in a taxi, rather than burping soda water in a minibus. Also it seemed like the wrong time of day.

Perhaps I showed my bewilderment.

"You don't worry for anything," said the driver. "I live here twenty-five years. You take number of car, and you can tell police."

He smiled again, sure that everything had now been happily taken care of. We drove away and stopped after a few minutes outside a shop. Curtains were drawn across the window on the inside. On the outside a sliding steel grille, used to lock up the shop from wall to wall, was almost closed, barely leaving access to the narrow door. We trooped silently into a stark square room with painted cement walls and ceiling, lit by a fluorescent tube. The shock made me wonder what I had been expecting. Plush? Piano music? Bawdy songs? Chandeliers? A deep-bosomed madam in a ballgown? The collection of tawdry old images, left to gather the dust of decades in my mind's attic, was suddenly and cruelly exposed by the demolition squad.

In front of the curtain, on a stand, a television set was yattering quietly in Thai, showing pictures of a refrigerator and a proud housewife. On rows of hard chairs ranged against two of the walls the girls sat in silence watching the TV. Our escort waved us to an empty wooden bench against the remaining wall. The centre of the room was bare. We might have been waiting for the dentist.

The girls looked quite lifeless, though they turned their heads as if to prove that they were, in fact, alive. They were all very young. I could not have said how young, and it may be that they had no idea either. The Swiss and I said not a word. The Norwegian jerked his head from one end of the row to the other and ground out some meaningless jokes which served rather to deepen the silence. The girls wore ordinary working clothes. Only the make-up on their puffy faces conceded anything to the kind of work they might be called upon to do.

The Swiss glowered at them. I fidgeted in embarrassment. Then the Norwegian stood up, cleared his throat, muttered something negative, and we followed him out to the bus. We drove to two more such places. They were almost identical, as were the girls, except that there were shelves on the walls crammed with cuddly toys. In these scenes of fearful boredom, my sense of revulsion and pity struggled to survive but finally succumbed. At the last stop, where the Norwegian was clearly determined to give the goods an even longer and more detailed scrutiny, I borrowed his copy of *Newsweek* and distracted myself thankfully from the miserable business.

After some time, I looked up from the magazine and noticed one girl who was prettier than the others. She might have been any age from twelve to sixteen. She was fondling a toy chicken in her lap, her eyes withdrawn and dreamy. For a moment I played with the old brothel-reformer's fantasy of paying the fee and offering my services as a platonic confidant and counsellor, but caught myself out instantly, having plumped for the pretty one.

She was not pretty enough for the Norwegian, evidently. Nor were the others. With a sigh, he gave up. The girl of tonight's dreams was not there. Our guides, forever solicitous, said we must visit "The Bungalow." That was where the best girls were: "Very expensive."

By now I had become genuinely curious to see what, if anything, would satisfy the Norwegian's yearnings. When he asked what I thought, did I want to go, I said, "Sure. Why not. If it's not too far."

"No. No. Not too far," said the Thai. "Just on edge of town."

The "bungalow" was a modern two-storey villa in a suburban garden. As we walked into the lounge, the Thai pimp told us that his star attraction had not yet come home from school. I asked why she was doing this work. He explained politely that she needed the money to buy her schoolbooks. I felt free to believe whatever I liked.

She came in soon afterwards from the kitchen and sat down on a sofa, demurely folding her hands on her pleated navy blue skirt. She had white-skinned clean features, a faint moustache, and a dazzling smile. The Norwegian looked at her uneasily. I thought his resistance was remarkable. There were two other women in the kitchen, and one of them came through to walk upstairs.

"That one I like," said the Norwegian. "How much is she for one night?"

She was obviously older, perhaps nineteen or twenty, and her skin was a more natural colour for a Thai. Next to her, all the "little girls" we had seen seemed to belong to a world of sickly fantasy which presumably satisfied the Thai philanderer's erotic ideal. I had to grant the Norwegian some grudging and limited respect for holding out.

He struck a bargain quite quickly, at twenty dollars, and she got into the bus with us. She seemed an ordinarily nice person, with little English and therefore little to say to us. The Norwegian tried his strangely fractured conversation on her and I tried to speak to the Swiss, but he could not take his eyes off the girl. I left the three of them in the restaurant and went upstairs to wash. When I came down they had disappeared.

I stepped out for dinner and to catch up with my journal over a beer before retiring to my room. The night was unpleasantly hot, and the room full of mosquitoes and dank odours from the alley. I dreamed a great deal, woke frequently and wondered about the Norwegian and his girl. When I heard sounds on the landing I got up, impelled partly by curiosity and partly by the need to relieve myself. I came out just in time to see the girl slip back through a door into one of the rooms.

I woke up early, anxious to get away. Should I say goodbye? As I paid my bill, I asked where the Norwegian was.

"Upstair. Sleeping.""

"Ah," I said. "And the Swiss?"

"Same thing."

"Which room?"

"Same room."

"Oh," I said, and left.

*

It had so often happened on my journey that after an unpleasant or disturbed night, instead of feeling tired and reluctant to face the day I was all the more confident and eager to get going. It was as though the purpose of the night was less to refresh the body than to give the mind its chance to flush out contradictions and frustrations. In the mornings after those long, dark hours of restlessness and vivid dreams, I had the clear impression that in some obscure chamber of the mind a loud debate had taken place, with heated argument, manoeuvring, and mudslinging, and that at the eleventh hour the different sides had triumphantly hammered out an agreement. I took my dreams to be the evidence presented by the parties to the dispute.

They were different from the dreams I had had in earlier life, in which I was left powerless in the face of some predicament. I still found myself in dangerous situations and awful figures from

my past still loomed up to threaten me, but I was able to overcome the dangers, and the dreaded "authorities" either crumbled
or became benign.

This busy and encouraging nightlife had continued as a vigorous
counterpoint to all the excitement of the days since my journey
had begun. It filled me with the hopeful belief that while I was
traveling with such exhilaration around the physical globe I was
also journeying much more freely through my own past and its
buried memories, and perhaps even reconstructing my own history to accord more usefully to the realities of the world as I registered them day by day. In fact, I deliberately let the events of the
night influence my progress directly, by trying as far as possible
to make my practical decisions in the morning according to how
I felt, rather than to a preconceived plan. This was an extraordinary luxury, denied to all but the most privileged and the most
primitive. I knew it and revelled in it. This exceptional chance to
lead a completely integrated life in which waking and sleeping, the
conscious and the unconscious, were so closely joined, gave me a
great incentive to keep going.

The mental ferment began to subside in Australia, when I tried
to share my journey with another person, and it collapsed alto-
gether in Penang. Now as I rode away from Haad Yai in the fresh
morning air I felt the first faint bubbling of that familiar excitement. Nothing like the full-blooded rush of joy I had been used to,
but a taste and a hope.

In all the events at Haad Yai I had been nothing more than a voyeur, a passive and, I thought, rather disreputable observer of other people's peculiarities on the seedy fringes of a decaying culture.

Yet I had come away with pages of jottings in my notebook, and a mind too busy with speculation to dwell on its own miseries. I realized that since my accident I had made hardly any notes, and this new beginning gave me added encouragement.

The world around me, as always, answered to my mood. Where the previous day the road had seemed dull and repetitive, today it blossomed with interest. The landscape and its people came alive for me, and I absorbed the changes since Malaysia. The painted wooden houses of Malaya, with their mouldings, decorations and other refinements, were gone. Here the village houses were bamboo wattle and daub with thatched roofs, long simple structures with their own natural beauty.

The roads were quieter. Ox carts, water buffalo, the paddy fields all around indicated farming on a smaller scale, and the peasant's frugal concern with every square foot of productive soil gave the landscape the neat, jewelled appearance of a painting in miniature.

There were few cars, some trucks, many bicycles, and quite a number of small motorcycles. These last amazed me by the use they were put to. It became common to see an entire family squeezed on to one little Honda or Yamaha; two adults with a child on the tank; the same with another child clinging at the back; the same with yet another child perched on the handlebars; and finally, my personal best sighting, three adults and two children glued together like Siamese quins on top of a hardly visible machine.

My aim that day was to get to Phuket on the west coast and then to find a place called Kata Beach. A mild-mannered young German traveler called Hans-Georg had first told me about it in Penang. I had formed an instant and instinctive liking for him and trusted his judgement. Phuket was an island some 150 miles north of Haad Yai, connected by bridge to the mainland, with many beaches, some busy, some almost deserted. Kata Beach, he said, was quiet and beautiful, and I imagined myself recovering there the wholeness that I had lost.

Some of the physical queasiness was already leaving me. I had the motorcycle to thank for that. One would not suppose that sitting on the saddle in a fixed position for hours on end would offer much in the way of exercise. It might even be thought a rather constricting and constipating form of inactivity, inclined to shake one's blood into one's boots, and rattle the vertebrae in an unhealthy manner, but curiously enough it has the opposite effect. All the muscles are in constant, if imperceptible, use to relieve the discomfort, and the vibration always seems to have a good effect on my digestion.

Those were the physical benefits of riding, but it also had the great negative virtue of removing me from the temptations of ginger beer and other sops craved by an idle and discontented mind.

In the afternoon I passed among some rock formations unlike anything I had seen before. They rose up abruptly from the undulating fields, pillars of stone as tall as a house, as though each one had been punched out of the earth's crust from below by one mighty blow still with its cap of topsoil and vegetation intact. The trees, bushes and grasses burgeoning on their crowns and dangling over their sides in such thick green luxuriance looked, from a distance, like immense wigs on supporting pedestals and conjured up images of some ancient race of giants. As they became more numerous and closer together the road rose and cavorted among them in ever-tightening curls. These gyrations tested the handling of the Triumph to the limit and I finally realized that my uneasiness on the bike was not just a subjective phenomenon, as I had imagined, but that there really was something wrong.

When I found that the alignment of the rear wheel was hopelessly out and corrected it, the bike seemed to jump forward like an animal released from a snare, and my confidence leaped forward with it.

So I arrived in Phuket stronger and happier than I had felt in weeks. Kata Beach was not easy to find. The road signs were in Thai, and my questions were met with polite incomprehension. Whichever way I tried to pronounce Kata it meant nothing to anyone, but I guessed my way and was lucky and found the dirt track which led me five miles across the island to the far shore just before dusk.

The first sight of Kata delighted me. From the brow of the last hill, I saw the beach below me in the shape of a broad smile between two promontories. The sand was bright and clean; the sea—green in its shallows, blue in its depths—was on fire from the setting sun. Coconut palms clustered above the high-tide mark, shading a broad strip of flat ground between the beach and the hills.

I followed the track down to the beach. Where it turned off to the left stood a rudimentary cafe or bar; a few tables on an earthen floor enclosed by a low wooden balustrade and sheltered by thatch. I stood the bike against the trunk of a palm and as soon as the engine noise stopped I felt at peace.

One of three men sitting in the cafe rose to welcome me in modest English.

"How do you do? Would you like a drink?" he asked.

I could not tell whether he was the proprietor, or whether it was a friendly invitation from a guest. I settled for a glass of tea which would not be of sufficient consequence to matter either way.

We sat at a table and exchanged a few questions and answers, diffidently, as the twilight gathered about us and the lamps were lit. I knew two things about Kata. At one end of the beach, Hans-Georg had said, lived a schoolmaster, a nice man who spoke English and had a little hut to rent. At the other end of the beach lived a French woman called Adrienne who was worth knowing. I had already guessed that I was sitting with the schoolmaster, and before asking him about his hut I said:

"Do you know someone called Adrienne?"

He looked out into the night and, quite innocent of the theatrical effect, pointed and said:

"There she is coming now."

I looked up, startled to see two headlights approaching through the palms. I walked out of the hut and waved my hand at the Datsun pickup as it appeared. There were four people in it, two women in the front and a couple in the back.

A woman with coppery gold hair and strong, regular features was driving. She stopped beside me and examined me with a pleasant, expectant look.

"Excuse me," I said. "Are you Adrienne?"

"Yes. Can I help you?"

Her question was deliberate, not perfunctory, and warmly put with a slight French accent. Instead of the neutral or defensive tone I expected, and which would have seemed natural, her voice implied an actual interest in my circumstances. Her initiative surprised me, heightened my senses, and left me a little flustered and awkward.

"Well, a friend of mine told me, er, suggested that I might try to get in touch. Hans-Georg? Do you remember? A German? He was here a few weeks ago?"

It was obvious that the name meant nothing to her. I stumbled to a halt, and my awkwardness increased.

"Never mind," she said. "Tell me, are you staying here?"

"Well, I would like to stay a few days. I haven't seen anything yet ... I mean, I've only just arrived and..." Really, I thought, this has got to stop. I'm behaving like an adolescent on his first trip abroad.

She took me off the hook very easily.

"We are just going to eat some fish on the beach. Would you like to come?"

"That would be wonderful. Gosh. Are you sure...?"

"Yes. Of course."

The reassurance was calm, and unequivocal. My own dithering responses embarrassed me but, more than that, they revealed how far I had drifted into confusion. Then I felt a sudden and profound sense of relief.

"Is it far?" I asked. "Shall I follow you? I'm on a motorcycle."

"You can leave it here and get in with us. It will be all right."

To leave the bike and everything on it was something I never normally did without a great deal of thought. It was my tribute to this woman and the occasion that I believed her and climbed unhesitatingly into the back of the Datsun. She introduced me to her son, Dan, a heavy young man who acknowledged me in an offhand way, and his girlfriend Karen, an American in her late teens.

They had little to say to me as we bounced along the rough track. It was a lovely, warm night. I leaned back, gripping the side of the pickup and watched a big moon sail among dramatic bars of cloud, brushed by the black silhouettes of palm fronds. I had the pleasant feeling that everything was happily settled and I was content to keep to myself for a while. There would be plenty of time for talking later.

The only one of us who spoke much was the girl, Karen. Or rather she did not so much speak as utter. She had evidently been complimented on the beauty and sensitivity of her utterances, because she produced them with an assurance that was quite unnatural for her age and completely unjustified by what she said. She had also dressed to suit the part, but her makeup and her elaborate ethnic clothes were out of place, and the prominent Indian headband was an overstated affectation of a "hippy" idea I was sure she could not understand.

All the way, she strained after her verbal butterflies, but caught only bats.

"The sky," she announced, "is like Beethoven's Fifth Symphony."

And you, I wanted to say, are like Herb Alpert playing it.

She buzzed and crackled on through the evening as disturbing as a faulty generator that produces no light. Dan cheered her on, appearing to marvel. For him she was Donovan in drag.

We arrived eventually at a small restaurant, and sat around a wooden table embedded in the sand to order shrimps, fish, rice, and vegetables. The third woman, who had been sitting next to Adrienne in the cab, was introduced to me as Alice. She was a blonde Jewish girl of about thirty, and she responded to my few polite questions with suspicion and a touch of hostility. I gathered that she was Australian and had run away from her family to live and study in Israel. Her manner provoked me into saying that I had been twice to Israel and had found the people too harsh for my taste, a remark which confirmed her in her poor opinion of me. She turned to Adrienne and engaged her with a loud monologue about Hong Kong and the fashion industry, praising and condemning everything and everyone in the most lavish terms.

Adrienne smiled gently and after a while took advantage of a pause to ask me where I had come from on my bike. I said I had come from England.

Alice pointed her forceful jaws at me and cried:

"*What* did you think of Nepal? Wasn't it the *most?* I mean, didn't it just *freak you out?*"

"I haven't been there yet."

"Oh, but you *must*. It's the most *incredible* thing."

"Yes. I. . ."

"And you *must* go trekking, because that is *totally and completely amazing.* Go on the Annapurna route, and you *must* fly up to Namche Bazaar if you can afford it and visit the *genuine* Tibetan communities."

"Well, I. . ."

"Oh, and you should *absolutely* go to Kopan, you know, the monastery? It's a Mahayana monastery. You could stay there a few days. Ask for Nick. He's a *really amazingly wonderful person.*"

"Nick?"

"He's a Mahayana monk."

"Nick the monk. What's there to do?"

"The best thing to do is meditation. It's *really outstanding.* You know. The quiet. I mean. It'll *really freak you out. Totally.*"

This last, delivered at almost screaming pitch, was a bit too much to take. The moon dived behind the cloud, and I couldn't hear the waves any more.

"Is that what you did up there?"

I didn't try too hard to hide my incredulity. She was noisy, almost hysterical, but she was sharp, too.

"Yes," she said shortly. "Have you finished with the fish?"

Karen was gazing rapturously to sea.

"I think I see George Harrison walking in on the waves," she murmured. "I mean I can almost see it, can't you?"

"Yay," said Dan. "Right on."

Adrienne asked me what kind of journey I was making and I had to say that I was "going round the world on a motorcycle." I hated the phrase. It always sounded supremely silly to my ears.

"Then which way have you come so far?"

I explained in as few words as possible. I found I could hardly bear to talk about my own adventures because of the sense of disgrace I still carried with me from Penang. It was like being asked to recall the sweetness of a honeymoon during the bitterness of a divorce. I felt terrible pangs of loss and regret for the first lyrical years of my journey, and feared that such joy could never be recovered. To the others I must have seemed a recalcitrant, rather arrogant man for withholding so much.

"Down through Africa," I said, "then round South America and up to California. Then round Australia and up from Singapore."

"How long has that taken you?"

"Well, it's nearly three years now."

"And how many kilometres is that?"

Adrienne was softly persistent, and I began to feel better about it.

"In miles it's just over forty-four thousand, on the bike that is. So that would be about seventy thousand kilometres."

"A long way," she said. "You must have learned a lot."

"It's impossible not to," I said, though I did not really believe that. There were blind travelers, and stupid ones too.

"You must sometimes have wished you could just stop and go home. No?"

"No," I said. "Never. I have never wanted to stop, even at the worst moments."

I surprised myself with my own vehemence. *It's true,* I thought, *nothing will make me stop. So it must be all right, if I believe in it that much. Really, I already owe this woman a lot.*

Alice was fidgeting belligerently, and burst out:

"Where were you in California? I mean, you must have passed right by Esalen. Did you go?"

"No, I didn't go. I've heard a lot about it. Encounter groups, stuff like that?"

Alice of course had been there. She had, in fact, submitted herself to an impressive array of healing influences. She had visited ashrams, monasteries, shrines, and temples of counter-culture. She had rubbed shoulders with gurus, monks, and the acknowledged heroes of alternative medicine, Feldenkrais and Govinda among them. She adulated them. She spoke of them with shrill awe. She heaped her praise upon them all. "Hallelujah," she shouted, "for they are all totally amazing and incredible and completely powerful high-energy people," and "Glory be," she sighed, "for I am freaked out."

Unhappily, they must have missed Alice with their high-energy beams of enlightenment as she prostrated herself before them. She had succumbed, while traveling, to a combination of sickness and heartbreak, and it was Adrienne who had gathered her up from the wayside like a stricken bird. She had been convalescing at Kata for several weeks and had already recovered most of her vitality, which was of a high order but of the kind that is self-consuming. Behind her square, intelligent, and somewhat greedy face I imagined a girl who believed that unless she shouted very loudly she would cease to exist.

We continued talking for some time, Alice with more pugnacious accounts of miracles she had perceived and charismatic geniuses she had befriended, Karen with ever more painful failures to grasp the muse, I with increasingly acerbic judgements and refusals, and Dan with occasional ponderous betrayals of ignorance. It struck me that, with the exception of Adrienne, we were a pretty disagreeable and unsatisfactory lot. Yet, oddly enough, we coexisted and, for all our antipathies, we were even enjoying ourselves. This triumph of mediation was achieved by Adrienne. Throughout our displays of belligerence, pomposity, sulking, and affectation, she gazed with equal and unmistakable fondness on all of us and radiated a peaceful glow that had some authority too. The calming influence of the sea and the stars seemed to flow through her, and the great warm night above our little lamp-lit table drew out our silly fears and spites and soaked them away.

I envied Adrienne her composure. She had that combination of sensitivity and detachment which I was so anxious to recover and I was very glad when she asked if I would like to stay with them. I was curious to know the source of her strength, since it was obvious to me that it had come as the result of prolonged effort and determination.

I found the motorcycle just as I had left it, and I followed the others to the far end of the beach. Between the palms we passed more huts, some lit by fluorescent tubes, some by oil lamps. Through the shadows figures in sarongs moved softly about and among them I saw the quiescent mass of a water buffalo, sleeping.

Raised in London by a German mother and a Romanian father, Ted Simon found himself impelled by an insatiable desire to explore the world. It led him to abandon an early career in chemical engineering to go to Paris, where he fell into journalism.

On 6th October 1973, at the age of 42, Ted set off from London on a 500cc Triumph Tiger motorcycle on what became a four-year solo journey around the world, covering 64,000 miles through 45 countries.

With the aim of discovering how the world had changed in the intervening 28 years, on 27th January 2001, aged 69, Ted embarked on a second journey. This time he rode a BMW R80 GS over 59,000 miles through 47 countries.

Ted's books about his journeys, Jupiter's Travels, Riding High, and Dreaming of Jupiter *continue to serve as an inspiration to other travellers who seek to know the world, and their place in it, through personal adventure.*

🌐 *Jupitalia.com*
🌐 *JupitersTravellers.org*

RUNNING OUT OF "SOMEDAYS"

By Jeremy Kroeker

Like many Canadians, I'm quietly proud of the wild territory that looms in our North. Perhaps we don't think about the Arctic all that much, but sometimes it whispers to us from the back of our minds, "I'm here," and we get goosebumps. After all, we are the true North, strong and free. Yet most of us live huddled against our southern border with the U.S. like so many field mice against a hot-water pipe. We don't want to be Americans, you see, but sometimes we want their climate.

Yet, the Arctic calls. For me, it was never a question of whether or not I'd venture north of the 60th parallel, but when. I'll do it someday, I told myself. Someday.

Then it dawned on me that none of us know how many "somedays" we have left. Even now, at the age of 43, I'm fairly sure that there are more "somedays" behind me than "somedays" that lie ahead. Another certainty: every time I missed the short weather window for riding motorcycles in the north, I missed an entire year. Simple math, really, but this year it hit home.

It hit home because my friend, Nevil Stow, was planning a ride to the Arctic this summer as a memorial to his brother Andy, who had recently passed away. Thus, on a wintery night in Canmore,

Alberta, while drinking margaritas (as usual) with Nevil in his warm garage, I decided that I would join him on his trip.

Actually, I probably slurred that I wanted to, "(expletive deleted) go to the (expletive deleted) Arctic with you. (Expletive deleted.)" This is why I have a phone case with a quote from Hemingway that reads, "Always do sober what you said you'd do drunk. That'll teach you keep your mouth shut." Well, following that advice has taught me nothing.

Anyway, tagging along on Nevil's trip would be easy. Nevil had made most of the arrangements already, including assembling a small team. Joining us would be Nevil's cousin, Nick Carter, who was flying in from England for the trip. Nick normally rode a Harley-Davidson, as he reminded almost everyone with whom he spoke, but for this trip he would take a borrowed BMW R 1200 GS. Nick was a stocky man, heavily tattooed, with a shaved head and a grey beard. He had all the swagger and mannerisms of a badass biker, but he was funny, and easy to have around.

Then there was Dave Booth, who lived in Canmore. Standing next to Nick, Dave looked like someone had fastened a t-shirt to an assembly of yardsticks. Dave is a former long-distance runner and extreme alpinist who served in the British Royal Air Force. His mental catalogue of lewd jokes and ditties is astonishing, and he would have us alternately laughing or cringing at nearly every stop. He would be riding his own BMW R 1200 GS.

And, let's not forget Nevil himself. Nevil walks with a bowlegged strut, shoulders pushed back, chest out, unruly hair blowing about, and usually casting a smile through a reddish-grey goatee. For this trip, he would be riding an old, but well-maintained, Suzuki DR650 named Twiggy—the same machine that he used to ride a lap around the world in 2013.

Together, on a warm June day, the four of us set off from Canmore, with me astride my overburdened Kawasaki KLR650. It was overburdened because Nevil made me bring spare tires. Although, yes, I did use them during the trip, I'm pretty sure that Nevil made me bring tires so that I could not bring my guitar. The last time he heard me play, I only knew "Peaceful, Easy Feeling," and he refuses to allow that I've progressed in the past two years.

The bike was also overburdened because I must haul litres of spare engine oil. Even riding annoyingly slowly and holding up the team, my 2008 KLR would demand eight litres of oil over the course of our 8,000 kilometre round trip (not counting an oil change). I could get the rings fixed, but I prefer treating the symptoms rather than the problem—the same policy I apply to every aspect of my life.

Our route, as mapped out by Nevil, would take us from Canmore, Alberta (near Calgary), through Jasper, Alberta and Smithers, BC, then north along the Stewart-Cassiar Highway to Watson Lake in Yukon. From there, we would travel through Whitehorse, Dawson City, up and over the Top of the World Highway past Chicken, Alaska to Fairbanks, and, finally north again along the Dalton Highway—a mud road that thinks it's a highway—to Coldfoot, Alaska, just north of the Arctic Circle.

Cobalt skies, teal lakes, and aqua-blue glaciers punctuated our short ride to Jasper, where we camped at the Wapiti Campground. It was this first night that I became aware of two problems:

1. My teammates were English or, in Dave's case, had spent so much time in England as to adopt the mannerisms of an Englishman. This meant that I would spend most of my time around the campfires befuddled. Technically, we all spoke the same language, but they said things like, "Bog roll," "Wizard prang," and "My mother was billeted at Cranwell." Utter nonsense.

2. Although these men were older than me, they could all drink booze like CFL offensive linemen. And they would still be up at 6:00 am, packed and loaded by 7:00, and ready to ride by 7:30. Actually, they could be ready much sooner if they weren't all trying to pretend like they weren't in a hurry.

Problem number two became obvious one day when shouting outside my tent jolted me awake. The previous night had been one of excessive libation, one in which I had wandered off to scale an iron bridge along the highway. When my whiskey bottle fell out of my pocket (like Maverick, I had been "inverted"), and tumbled, bouncing off the bridgework onto the riverbank below, I suddenly realized that this—this—is exactly how drunken people die. I climbed back down and joined my friends at the fire.

Anyway, I awoke the next day to shouting. "Jeremy! Time to get up!" someone called. I poked my head out of the tent to see the trio had already broken camp, packed, eaten breakfast, and donned their motorcycle gear. It was 7:30, after all. This meant that, although we were all physically in the same location, they were at least an hour ahead of me. That was a lesson to us all. From then on I would set an alarm, and if I ever did oversleep (which never happened again) they would try a little harder to wake me, and sooner.

In spite of Nevil's nearly constant reminders that "it always rains on the Cassiar Highway, gentlemen," we rode the full length of the Cassiar Highway in nearly perfect weather, rolling through vast swaths of burned timber, to reach Watson Lake and the famous Signpost Forest. After snapping a few obligatory photos, the following exchange occurred between Nevil and me. I include it here simply to illustrate how infuriating a travel partner I can be. This is due to, not a head injury as it would seem, but my inability to pay attention when people are speaking ... especially when I'm doing the math to figure out if I need fuel or not.

"Where's the next fuel stop?" I said.

"Rancheria Lodge," Nevil replied.

"How far is that?"

"Maybe 150 kilometres."

"And what's the place called?"

"Rancheria."

"And how far is it?"

"So, maybe 150 kilometres, more or less."

"I'm sorry. What's it called?"

"Rancheria."

"And ... so, it's like ..."

"150 kilometres."

"Okay. And, this place ... it's called what now?"

At this point, Nevil threatened to push over my motorcycle and rugby tackle me.

Running west, we stopped at Rancheria Lodge for fuel ("What's this place called?" I shouted to Nevil as we pulled up). We snapped down a quick meal before pushing on to Teslin. There we rolled across a long iron bridge deck. These metal-grate bridges hum and whine beneath your tires and cause your machine to off-track a bit, giving the feeling of riding in sand. They're safe enough, though, and if you can relax, you can glance down past your feet and the see the water directly below.

Finally, we arrived at Whitehorse, Yukon, where we camped at Takhini Hot Pools for two nights. This would be our first rest day after over 2,000 kilometres, and we spent it touring the Yukon Beringia Interpretive Centre, where they have impressive fossils of woolly mammoths on display.

Our next rest day occurred in Dawson City. Unlike Whitehorse, with its big-box stores and modern feel, Dawson City feels more like the stereotype of gold-rush north country, with its grey board-walks and wide dirt streets. The shops, bars, and hotels feature wood siding and squared-off facades with hand-painted signs.

A free ferry churned against the swift current of the Yukon River, carrying us crablike across the water to the Yukon River Campground, where we stayed for two nights. The first night, around the campfire, I made it very clear to everyone that, no, I did not intend to get up at 6:00 am to go for a ride. Not at all, in fact. Was I sure? Yes. Getting up at six and riding is what we had been doing every day since leaving Canmore. No, on this day I intended to sleep in and, to my surprise, the guys allowed it. The next day, although I did hear the motorcycles start up, I enjoyed a wonderful morning snoozing and reading.

When I finally rolled out of my tent, I wandered back to the ferry, crossed the river and strolled into town. There I found the real gem of the Yukon. I had been told to track down a little bar colloquially known as "The Pit," and I was not disappointed.

Located on the ground floor of the pink, clapboarded Westminster Hotel, The Pit is the epitome of a dive bar. It's clean, though, and populated with characters that would fit into any poem by Robert W. Service. The ceiling and floors slope in all directions (even when you're sober), and old paintings in mismatched frames decorate the walls between the stuffed heads of one animal or another.

It was at The Pit that I began my search for the best Caesar in Dawson City, and I had my work cut out for me. By the time the guys caught up with me late in the afternoon, I had walked to about six or eight bars, and I was back at The Pit. From there, we went to the Sourdough Saloon for a Sourtoe Cocktail, a strange beverage consisting of any hard liquor (usually Yukon Jack) and garnished with a mummified human toe. If you wish to join the "Sourtoe Cocktail Club" (and who doesn't?) there is only one rule:

"You can drink it fast, you can drink it slow, but your lips must touch the toe."

The next day we crossed into Alaska via the Top of the World Highway. This high-elevation northern track is only open in the summer, and even then, snow can remain in shady hollows along the way much of the year. It started to rain as we crossed the border, and the gravel path got slick, but we made it to Tok, Alaska without mishap.

After a night in Fairbanks, we rode north again along the Dalton Highway, finally closing in our goal of reaching the Arctic Circle. We found the Dalton in slick, muddy condition, which is not unusual. As my bike was still overburdened with spare tires and litres of oil, I suffered through several sphincter-clenching moments per hour as my front tire slipped out in the mud. Sometimes a track would catch my wheel and I'd just have to go where the track took me, and sometimes the mud was too soft to leave tracks, and that made turning a chore as well. But we all kept up on our wheels.

As I took up the rear, visibility was the real problem. Each bike in front of me, and every other passing vehicle, lifted a gritty spray into the air that seemed to hang just long enough to attach itself to my visor. With no choice but to wipe it clear so I could see, I left hundreds of horizontal scratches in the plastic. After an hour or so, I was peering out through a clear patch about the size of a credit card.

Swiping across my visor yet again, I noticed a sign warning motorists against stopping on the long Yukon River Bridge (official name: the E.L. Patton Bridge). The bridge slopes down across the water, and its deck is made of wood. In these conditions, the signs were unnecessary: stopping would have been impossible. Again, my front tire slipped out a few times and, when I geared down to scrub some speed, my rear tire began to skid. It seemed like we were on a frictionless plane and the only thing keeping us upright was the centrifugal force of our wheels.

The road and the weather improved somewhat after the bridge, and we made good time through the rolling landscape of boreal forest, Arctic meadows, and mountains. And then, just south of our intended campsite in Coldfoot, Alaska (pop. 10), we found the little pullout that marks the 60th parallel, the Arctic Circle.

We rolled in and parked our bikes in front of the sign. In proper English style, handshakes were proffered, along with modest congratulatory remarks and whiskey. We each had a wee dram and shared a few laughs while snapping photos before getting serious for a moment.

This was a memorial ride, after all, and it was time to toast the departed. Nevil's brother Andy had been a teetotaler for most of his life, but when the tumour that grew in his brain began affecting his personality, he suddenly and inexplicably began drinking spiced rum. And so, Nevil produced a bottle of spiced rum here at the Arctic Circle, toasted his brother, and poured out a portion into the mud. Then we all took a swig from the bottle as our thoughts turned to mortality and, in this moment, how good it was to be alive. We also found ourselves wishing so hard that Andy had chosen a different libation in his final days. That rum was horrible.

Having completed our objective, all that remained was to reach Coldfoot, set up camp, and get some food. That night we discussed our options. We had heard from other riders that the road north to Deadhorse, Alaska, the final stop on the Dalton Highway, was under construction and in extremely poor condition. It would probably take us three days to get up there, take some photos of a few ATCO trailers, and backtrack to Coldfoot. In the end, we decided that reaching the Arctic Circle was the real prize, and that pushing on just to say we had reached the end of the road wouldn't be worth it. We could put those three days to better use on some of our favourite roads in BC.

The next day we packed up (I was still carrying my spare tires), and headed south. We stopped again at the rest area with the Arctic sign, but we only paused briefly. I looked down at the spot where Nevil had poured out some rum and I reflected on the motivation for this trip.

I didn't know Nevil's brother, and I probably would have joined Nevil and the guys even if it hadn't been a memorial ride—as I've said, the Arctic calls—but embarking on an adventure because of a death gives both the adventure and the death extra meaning. Parting with loved ones is sad, but it serves as a powerful reminder to live life.

Every time I lose a friend, or someone dear to my heart loses someone, I'm reminded that I'm running out of "somedays," even as my list of things to do gets longer. At some point, my list will be impossible to complete, so it's wise to chip away at it while I can.

One day, instead of someone handing me the bottle, someone will pour my portion out onto the ground. I only hope that it's horrible whiskey that makes everyone wince and suck air through their teeth.

Here's to the departed. Now let's go for a ride.

Jeremy Kroeker is the author of Motorcycle Therapy, and Through Dust and Darkness.

- *MotorcycleTherapy.com*
- *@Jeremy_Kroeker*
- *@Jeremy_Kroeker*
- *@MotorcycleTherapy*

ME, GEORGE, AND AN AWESOME RIM JOB

By Ed March

It was July 2012, and I was in Ulaanbaatar, Mongolia with six riders
on seven Honda 90s. The previous year I'd got drunk at a motorcycle rally in the UK and decided I would lead a tour of people from
Mongolia to the UK: over 7,000 miles and two months, on bikes
with less than seven horsepower. Despite sobering up many times
after that rally, I still thought it was a good idea for some reason,
so after sending out the world's worst information pack, with an
intended route drawn in Microsoft Paint, I had six people sign up.
And here we were, in Mongolia—a country that is almost entirely
off-road—on bikes that most people wouldn't ride to the shops.

The mixture of people that signed up for this "guided tour" was
nothing short of spectacular, to be honest. I had a rider in the
teens, 20s, 30s, 40s, 60s and 70s, and from all walks of life, but
with a common quest for adventure. This story centres on the guy
in his twenties, George. George's reason for being on this tour was
the same tale I've heard a thousand times. At the start of each
year, he and his friends would be down the local pub deciding what
awesome adventure they would all be embarking upon this year.
It was going to be the best and most exhilarating quest they'd
ever dreamt up, and would surely be the antidote they needed to
put up with modern life and its dull 9-to-5 jobs. But every year,

one by one, George's friends would drop out, eventually leaving George with nothing but excuses from his mates to explain why no epic group adventure was going to be happening this year—and of course, ultimately, every year.

So here George was, in the capital city of Mongolia, with six people he'd never met before, about to start riding 7,000 miles back to the UK on a bike with a power output comparable to that of a decent toaster. George's bike, Jolene, had had a very hard life and, as those partial to an innuendo would say, had been ridden hard and put away wet. Her engine sounded tired and rattly, so I prodded around inside her (oh, grow up), and was rather horrified to find a 6.5mm socket inside her cam chain tunnel. What was even more worrying was that removing this socket made the noise much worse, so I put the socket back in. I then told George his bike was a piece of crap, and we'd just have to see how it would fare tackling some of the harshest terrain known to man.

In hindsight, this was probably not the best solution to the problem.

The bike made it 300 miles before breaking down. Three hundred ball-smashing, neck-jarring miles, off-road across the Mongolian steppe. We were now in the absolute middle of nowhere, Jolene was so down on power that she could barely pull the skin off a rice pudding, and the engine sounded like it was being dragged down the road instead of powering the bike. I got George to remove the engine casing, as the rumbling of the engine sounded so bad I assumed the problems lay in the very bowels of it. We didn't have a soft-faced mallet to tap on the engine to break the seal, so George

used the thigh bone of a dead cow that lay nearby, not much further than arm's reach from the scene of what felt like Jolene's final
breaths. He removed the casing. I looked inside, and yes, it was
terminal. The big-end bearing had failed. We had no idea why, but
it didn't matter. I took a step back, lit a thinking cigarette, and
started to contemplate what the next play was.

It had taken us three days to ride here. We'd come just far
enough to be too far to ride back to the capital city—the only place
where we stood a chance of getting a new engine to fix poor Jolene.
We were on the side of a hill, with nothing but rolling green grass,
rocks, and dead animals as far as the eye could see. There wasn't
a hope in hell of fixing this engine here. What was worse was that
we were on a time scale. We had eight weeks in total to ride back to
the UK, and even if the rest of the group was okay with riding an
extra 600 miles to the capital city and back, the time limit wasn't.

As I got to the end of my thinking cigarette, the true implications
of the situation had become clear to me, and rather heartbreak-
ingly, to George. George's trip was over, and he knew it. We reas-
sembled the engine, and asked Jolene to try and muster a few final
breaths to limp through the sand, mud, and rocks to carry George
to the nearest village. She could only do 10 mph by the end, but she
did get him there. But now was not the time for celebration.

On this long, slow ride to the relative safety of the village, George
had come to accept his fate. We found a spot in a guesthouse for
a group chat; it was time to discuss George's leaving the group. I
made eye contact with him, and I saw the exact same emotions of

that guy down the pub who had been let down by all his friends year after year. Only this time, his disappointment was being caused by an engine, not his mates.

George told the group that he would now abandon the bike in the village, get a taxi back to the capital city, and then fly home. He was gutted that his two-month adventure of a lifetime had been stopped after just three days of riding, but there was no alternative. The trip was over.

His logic was sound, but it just didn't feel right to me. We were on Honda 90s, and I've always said that nothing can stop a Honda 90. There was no way I was letting George's trip end like this. So I hatched a ridiculous but cunning plan. I would send the other riders off ahead on a predetermined route with all of my luggage. I would then jump in the taxi with George back to Ulaanbaatar to source a new engine. George was convinced this wouldn't be possible, even though I know you can find a Honda 90 engine anywhere in the world within a day.

This was where my plan got ingenious. If George was correct, and there was no engine when we got back to the city, he would fly back home as planned. I would get the free return journey in the taxi, then ride my unloaded bike at maximum speed to catch up with the rest of the group. However, if I was correct, we would buy an engine, both get the free return taxi ride back, do a quick engine change, and then both play catch-up.

George couldn't argue with this plan, as it still allowed his pessimistic premonition to happen if his non-engine-finding beliefs turned out to be true.

So it was settled. George went off to find a taxi that was prepared to do 600 miles off-road, and I talked to the rest of the group about what route they needed to take to ensure that I would be able to find them again in about three days' time. Once the route was set, I went outside to find what taxi George had scored. Oh my. It was a half-black, half-rust two-door 1960s Kamasa jeep. And, oh my god, was it knackered. It could only be started with a hammer, and I don't mean using it to hit the starter solenoid. As far as I could tell, the driver had to hit the injector pump with it. If that didn't work, he had to get underneath it and hit something else under there very hard, but I never found out what that part was.

"What's the driver's name?" I asked George.

"I don't know, actually, but he doesn't speak a single word of English," George replied with a comedic shrug, as if to say "300 miles with this guy is going to be interesting, isn't it?"

"Me: Ed. This: George. What is your name?" I said to the driver, with massively overemphasized gestures.

"Rim Job," the guy replied.

"Errr ... come again, old chap," I replied, trying to ignore George's childish sniggers.

"Rim Job!" the driver said again.

"Right, well, there we go, George, our driver is called Rim Job. That's actually a thing that's happening."

Time was really of the essence, so we said our goodbyes to the group, Rim Job took out his hammer and started whacking the engine bay, and I clambered into the back seat of what would be our home for the next 12 hours. And then 12 hours back.

"Oooh, the inside of the rear cabin has been lined and padded like a cell in a mental hospital, that's quite pretty," I said to George.

It turned out it wasn't there for looks, it was actually there for function. You see, the only thing this jeep was lacking more than functioning suspension was seat belts. And I was sitting right over the rear axle.

I don't think it's possible to ever convey just how bumpy this 12-hour journey was, but it was three years ago, and I think my eyes are still wobbling now.

I specifically remember one 100-metre section being so bad that I was repeatedly thrown up into the padded roof. When George finally let go of the dashboard and turned around to hear what all my shouting had been about, I was actually upside down in the seat with my head in the footwell and my feet pressed against the rear window. Needless to say, I was very thankful for the padded roof after that.

We had left at about 2 pm, and Rim Job did indeed do his job very well, driving until sunset, and then continuing on through the night in this vehicle that sounded like a piano being ridden down a cliff. He only stopped when the headlights went out so he could get out to hit them with a slightly softer hammer than the one used for the engine. At around 3 am or so, we made it to the city and stopped in a Mongolian tent village to sleep for what little remained of the night.

At 8 am our wakeup call happened in the form of Mr. Job using the trusty starting hammer on the jeep. The engine was running just the other side of the tent canvas, or inside my head, it was hard to tell. Never mind, it was time to get up, head to the bike market, and buy Jolene a new engine.

We got to the market, and ... oh, tits. The market is closed on Wednesdays. And Rim Job was leaving in two hours. Balls. Balls, balls, balls, balls. What would we do now?

George knew what he'd do. George would fly home.

It couldn't end like this. There must be another way. "There's a place around the corner that sells Chinese bikes out of a shipping container, maybe he's open!" I offered to George as a glimmer of hope.

We walked around the corner, and sure enough, he was open. Huzzah!!!

I took a calm walk through the bikes, trying to play it cool to the seller, and went back to George. "The second bike from the end, the blue one. Its engine will slot straight in your bike. It's a manual clutch, but it'll work. How much are you prepared to pay for it?" I said to George, while still trying to hide my excitement from the shop/container keeper.

"£500 was the price of the plane ticket, so £500 seems fair to me," George replied very logically.

After about a minute of haggling, the deal was done for £350, and I handed George the keys and registration documents to his new motorcycle.

Yeah. Rather annoyingly, we had to buy the complete motorcycle, as the vendor wouldn't sell just the engine. This was a bit of a pain because we had no tools to remove the engine with.

Our solution to this hiccup was to push it to the motorcycle-friendly camp-ground that we'd left four days ago. This place was filled with BMW and KTM riders stranded there, waiting for some sensor or complicated part to get mailed to them because Mongolia doesn't stock the parts for western bikes.

The guys in the campground were confused, to say the least. "What are you guys doing back here? Where's the rest of your group? Where are your bikes? Why are you pushing a brand-new Chinese motorcycle?" They all began asking, laughing more with each question.

"Don't have much time, need to drop the engine out of this bike in less than half an hour because Rim Job is leaving soon. Yes, our taxi driver is called Rim Job."

Once the sniggers died down, the standard question from a $20,000 motorcycle owner got asked. "You're gonna remove an engine in less than 30 minutes?"

"Yeah, of course I am, give me the right tools and it'll be done in ten," I replied, hoping that laying down this gauntlet to the bored bikers waiting for DHL would provoke them to get out their toolkits. And by Jove, it worked!

The engine was on the floor within 15 minutes, then loaded into the back of the jeep. The next problem was that we now had to abandon this Mongolian motorcycle, because it wouldn't be allowed across the border without huge export taxes.

I stood on top of the sturdiest table I could find. "Who wants to buy a brand-new motorcycle? It only has 0.5 kilometres on the clock, which is the distance we had to push it 30 minutes ago. Lovely condition, one careful owner."

The campground residents appreciated the humourous sales pitch, but they already had one broken bike each—why would anyone want another? There was nothing but silence.

"Come on, guys, it's brand new, it's got to be worth something?" I asked, trying not to sound too desperate, even though everyone knew we had to leave almost immediately. "Surely someone can offer something for it?"

And then an offer came from the back. "I'll give you breakfast for it!"

"What kind of breakfast?" George asked almost instantly, as if there were nothing weird about owning a brand-new bike for less than an hour before swapping it for food.

"Anything you want off the menu," the mystery voice shouted.

"Two lots of eggs and bacon on toast, and a bag of fizzy drinks for the return journey, and you've got a deal!" George replied, completely fine with this ridiculous situation.

"Done," said the mystery voice, now revealed to belong to the joint owner of the campground. He ordered our food from the kitchen, and within minutes George was ceremoniously handing over vehicle paperwork in one hand and receiving bacon in the other.

The deal was done and all the campground residents were thoroughly and understandably confused by what had just happened. We were metaphorically eating George's motorcycle, and Rim Job was once again smashing the granny out of the engine bay to start the diesel-powered shed on wheels that we were about to travel back to Jolene in.

Wicked! I thought. The plan actually worked!

I got back into the jeep (which now felt like one of those posh lined coffins) and Rim Job managed the perfect whack to bring life to the engine. We apologized to the campers for the horrific cloud of thick black smoke that engulfed the jeep, and commenced Operation Ball-Bash #2. The time was about 2 pm or so when the wheels started turning and we headed back into the desert again. Luckily, the drudgery of the relentless bouncing of our rattly transport was counteracted pretty effectively by looking at George's new engine sitting on the spare seat. We were winning the battle, but Jesus, was it bumpy! The sounds of the engine and suspension components banging together were so loud that conversations between George and me had to stay fairly simple, as any words longer than two syllables were unintelligible. We drove for hours until the sun started to set, shining directly in our eyes since we were heading west and only obscured by the occasional dust cloud. The sun eventually set, but of course we kept moving. At around midnight we stopped at a roadside shack for some snacks and a good leg-stretching. Alas, after 15 minutes it was time for us three to get back in the truck.

"Errr, George, there's a guy already in the back of the truck!" I said with a mixture of nervousness and humour.

"Rim Job ... this man ... okay?" I asked very slowly, once again deploying my overemphasized hand gestures.

"Okay," he replied, pointing for me to get in.

But things were not okay, not okay at all. The guy was enormous, well over six feet tall and half as wide, and once inside he started showing me photos of himself wrestling. But that wasn't the actual problem. The problem happened about 30 minutes into the journey.

"Errr, George," I said nervously, squashed between the tank of a man and the window. "The man is rubbing my leg up and down with his hand and smiling at me."

"Okay?" George replied in what was essentially laughter. I wasn't 100% sure what to do, but George is hairier than I am, so I asked for us to swap seats, hoping that his furry arms would put the wrestler off. We swapped seats and thankfully George didn't get abused.

Phew, problem solved.

I can't really tell you much about the rest of the journey, because after discovering that the front seat was much smoother than the rear one, I managed to fall asleep, and was awoken by the sound of tranquility, as at 5 am, our horrific mode of transport spluttered to a stop for the final time, and we were greeted by the sight of

Jolene and my bike, Ninety, against the beautiful backdrop of a Mongolian sunrise.

Now, I like burning the candle at both ends as much as the next chaos junky, but I couldn't face doing an engine change now. George and I said our goodbyes to Rim Job and the Mongolian wrestler, and went into the guesthouse to get a few hours' sleep. The sound of the alarm clock going off five hours later felt like it was being bashed into my face, but needs must, and we had a group of five bikers to catch up with.

George and I wobbled outside to the bikes, and set to work. Like a well-oiled machine (one that swore a lot and smelt like body odour and spilt Coca-Cola), we dropped the old, knackered engine out of Jolene, and slotted in the new one within the hour. One swift kick and the bike lived again! We looked at each other with a look that resembled disbelief.

"Holy shit! It works!" I proclaimed to George while he looked back at me gleefully. "We've got some catching up to do!"

The beauty of giving all my luggage to the rest of the group was that I could now take half of George's luggage, meaning that we are now on very lightweight bikes, way lighter than any of the bikes we were trying to catch up to. Add into the mix that fact that we were now both pumped to see how fast we could catch up with the other guys, and we had ourselves a nice little challenge unfolding.

With the bikes fired up and all the gear strapped down, we headed out into the trails and onto the route I had told the other guys to take. At our last radio contact, it had appeared that by tonight they should be 150 miles away and it had taken them basically three days to get there. Their only having done 50 miles per day meant the terrain had been very tough. And we would have to do much more.

Mission accepted! We both rode like absolute nutters. Both our bikes were getting airborne fairly regularly, which, considering some children's pushchairs have more suspension than we did, was no mean feat. I like things in life to have purpose, and this race was caked in it. We stopped only for fuel, chocolate bars, and Coca-Cola, knowing that as long as we rode like maniacs, we could really eat into the group's lead over us. There was no time to stop to check the map. I would just wait until a relatively smooth section of dirt and then check it, one-handed, while my right hand kept the throttle pinned to allow me to fly over potholes instead of crash into them.

The progress we made was absolutely staggering, and that night when we stopped, we were very impressed with how far away the other riders were. They were about one metre away, to be precise.

That's right, in just seven hours of riding, we had managed what they did in three days! I'd drunk so much Red Bull that I was convinced I could see time, and as we sat down to have our celebratory beer, George still seemed to be looking out for potholes, even though he wasn't even on a bike any more.

The conversation with the group was very entertaining, and a couple of beers helped calm George and me down. Recounting being sexually harassed by a Mongolian wrestler luckily didn't bring on any trauma, and swapping a motorcycle for breakfast seemed even more stupid now than it did the first time round. Many laughs were had, and questions answered, but it was well past our bedtime, and we had a lot of sleep to catch up on.

In the morning, as I staggered out of the hotel in a sleepy stupor, one of the guys brought me a cup of coffee, which I enjoyed as I sat down on a wooden step alone in the hotel courtyard. I began to wake up properly while looking at the now-complete line of seven Hondas in front of me.

After 15 minutes or so, George appeared from round the corner, having just eaten breakfast, and wandered over to me. He had a bit of a cheeky grin on his face as if to say, "Yeah, that's right, we did three days' riding in seven hours."

And as we both admired the rather symbolic lineup of bikes in front of us, he took the rare opportunity of our being alone to have a quick word with me. "I just wanted to say thanks for what you did for me. What you did was pretty mental, and you really went above and beyond to stop my trip from ending. You would have been completely within your rights just to let me fly home, and I would have been completely fine with that. But you didn't, you put yourself through hell for no real reason other than to ensure that I got to complete this trip. So I just wanted to say thank-you."

I wouldn't say I welled up inside, but I did feel a bit emotional. Because for a follow Englishman to say thank-you in such a heart-felt way, when no one else is watching, meant a lot. You see, we Brits don't often talk about our feelings like that. Like, we certainly don't hug each other until we've pretty much shared a near-death experience. Just a solid handshake with eye contact, thank you very much!

And I was very happy with what I'd done. This is why I ride around the world, to find new problems, and when 99% of people would run away and hide, I run straight towards it, balls-out, and solve it.

Was it a bit stupid to split the group into two and send them off into the unknown while George and I got the worst taxi I've ever seen; traversed the worst terrain I've ever seen; bought a motorbike just for the engine, then swapped it for eggs and bacon; then got hit on by the Mongolian Hulk before riding at ridiculous speeds across even more horrific terrain?

Damn right it was stupid! But life is stupid when you really think about it. Like it or lump it, we're all going to end up in a rocking chair at some point, facing death.

And when that day comes, all you'll have are memories. And when you pass away, all you'll be are memories. Some will see that sentiment as morbid, but I think it's completely the opposite: it's liberating. Get out there and do things that make you happy, do things that make other people happy, just DO THINGS!

You only get one shot at life, and when I'm in that rocking chair, I know I'm gonna be thinking, "Holy shit, what a ride!" And I'll happily raise a glass (or my colostomy bag) to my friend George, for being part of that episode of chaos.

Get out there and do stupid. You'll love it!

Ed March has one mission: To boldly take a pizza delivery bike where it really doesn't want to go: Iran, Mongolia, Russia, Vietnam, across Canada in the winter, the Arctic Circle in winter... The list of places is very long and often very stupid.

In 2011, Ed posted his faithful 85cc commuter bike, Ninety, to Malaysia and rode her home over 14,500 miles and eight months, all because someone dared him to. Since then, he's done about another 100,000 miles (the speedo cable broke in Iran in 2012, so it's anyone's guess, really) and visited 43 countries. He started making YouTube videos on the road to help share his experience of how awesome the world is, and to inspire others to get up and travel. The videos gathered more and more momentum until a feature film was released, and then a tour company was formed.

For some reason unknown to Ed, even after posting a YouTube video of himself licking a lamppost at -15°C and getting stuck to it for a worryingly long amount of time, people were still asking him to guide them on a tour.

The story in this book is from that first tour, and the first time Ed went to Mongolia.

🌐 *c90adventures.co.uk*
▶️ */c90adventures*
📘 */c90adventures*

THE RIDE HOME

By Mark Richardson

The three-week ride to the Pacific from Toronto took a toll on my old dirt bike. The clutch was worn out, the single shock absorber collapsed, the brakes touching steel on steel. I spent a week fixing her back into shape, staying with Ted Simon at his house north of San Francisco, before she was finally ready for the road again. Not great, but ready, so with a firm handshake of farewell and a head finally clear of cheap California wine, I kicked her into life and headed back east.

I was looking forward to this ride. I came out to the coast as a Pirsig Pilgrim, following the route of Robert Pirsig in *Zen and the Art of Motorcycle Maintenance*, and it was important to retrace the trail exactly. That ride became the basis for my book *Zen and Now*, in which I stayed at the same places and met some of the same people mentioned in Pirsig's classic 1974 story. On this ride home, however, I was my own boss again and could go wherever I wanted and stay wherever I liked. My wife and kids were away and the journey could take six weeks if I felt like it. I figured I'd stretch it all out over a month.

I rode east from Ted's house to Yosemite National Park and then headed south to the real objective: Death Valley. This was the third or fourth time I'd tried to make it to Death Valley—every previous ride ended prematurely with a breakdown of some sort, and I was concerned this might, too. The single air-cooled cylinder of the 20-year-old Suzuki DR600 tended to overheat and I was headed to the hottest place in North America—hell, the world, on many days—and this was mid-August and about as hot as it could get. I rode down from the cool hills of Yosemite to the dry, sun-bleached dirt of the desert and hoped for the best.

The bike was running okay, but she was grossly overloaded. I had a pair of heavy saddlebags, and then a Pelican case with a laptop and camera equipment lashed to the back rack. There was a dry bag on top of it with extra clothing, and if that had been all, I'd have been fine, but it was not: there was also a large bag that held a tent, camping gear, and the collapsed, heavy monoshock that I hoped to rebuild at home. The weight of that bag threw off the balance; I should have mailed it home, but I didn't want to risk losing it.

It took a couple of days to reach the northern access to Death Valley, and the heat seemed to build with every hour. I turned off the main highway somewhere near Mount Whitney and headed east, climbing a ridge of mountains. There was a lookout somewhere near the top and I pulled over to take a photo. The valley floor was white and looked intimidating. I was covered completely as protection from the sun, but not with the comfortable ventilated clothing of today: I was sporting a full-face helmet, jeans, boots, gloves, and a light leather jacket zipped to the top. Even here, high above the valley floor, it was hot, hot, hot. A minivan pulled over into the same lookout—the side door slid open and a couple of boys jumped out to take photos. "Close the damn door! You'll let the cool out!" called someone inside, but it didn't matter, because the boys threw themselves back in as soon as they felt the heat. The van pulled away, I zipped my jacket more tightly, pulled the silk scarf over my neck, and rode the highway down a thousand feet or so onto the valley floor.

It didn't take long to cross to the next ridge and begin rising again, and I was pleased to have conquered Death Valley. The heat was extraordinary, but the bike slogged on. I'd put synthetic oil in her at Ted's that allowed a higher running temperature, though if there'd been a problem, I'd have coasted to a halt beside the road with no shade and been screwed. If someone rescued me, I couldn't leave the bike because she'd probably be stolen by the time I returned; if I stayed for her, I'd roast. There was not a cloud in the sky and not a drop of moisture in the air. The place was a furnace, but I'd come out victorious.

Except that after climbing that ridge and reaching the top, another pullout offered another vista and I looked across a shimmering white valley floor that stretched to the horizon. There was no other side to this basin. That last strip of heat had only been an approach: Death Valley itself was blistering below.

It was only lunchtime. The plan had been to ride through and stay that night in Las Vegas, but I realized the naiveté of this as I dropped down and the heat grew. My scarf blew off and my neck started to burn. If anything happened to force a stop—anything at all—I'd be screwed.

Death Valley is a national park, and there's a community not far in called Stovepipe Wells. Nobody lives there permanently—it's a tourist stop, one of three managed by the private company that looks after the park for the parks service. There's a gas station with a gift shop and a motel with a restaurant and that's it. I pulled up to the motel registration office, went inside, and asked the cost of a room. Sixty bucks, said the clerk. Done, I said—I'd have paid six hundred. The room was just a few doors from the office and I went back out to move the bike in front of its door, but I couldn't pull in the clutch lever because it was so hot it burned my fingers. I put my gloves on, pushed the bike over, went inside and lay on the bed with the air conditioner blasting away. It was at least an hour before I could move.

When I finally got up, I walked across the street to the gas station to buy a cold drink. The thermometer in the shade above the door read 118°F.

*

The new plan was to leave at dawn and head for Vegas. At dawn, it would still be at least 100 degrees, but I'd be shielded from the intensity of the sun. I'd have ridden at night, except the bike's headlight wasn't strong and animals on the road were a very real danger. After dusk, I bought beer at the restaurant and sat on the porch watching the moon over the mountains. I was so happy to finally be there.

*

It was a comfortable ride the next morning, on a deserted high-way and with low light from the rising sun stretching my shadow out across the desert to the right. I rode south on the straight road and passed through Furnace Creek, then stopped at the Badwater Basin to appreciate the lowest point in North America. The altim-eter on my GPS agreed I was at 282 feet below sea level. There was nobody to be seen. I hung around until the heat began gaining strength, and by the time I reached Death Valley's southern exit, the sun was high in the sky again and the asphalt road was sticky against my boots. I thought the temperature would fall when I left the park, but it only dropped to maybe 115. By the time I reached Vegas, I was cooking again in my leather jacket.

A billboard on the approach to town advertised rooms for $20, and that sounded great, so I pulled off and rode to the motel's front office. It was a big place, with a pool and a casino, and I wanted a shower and some respite from the sun.

"Hello," I said to the clerk inside. "I'd like one of your $20 rooms, please."

"Certainly sir," said the clerk helpfully. "That'll be $60."

"What? How come it's not $20?"

"Those rooms are sold out for tonight, I'm afraid."

"Tell me—how many rooms do you have here?"

"Seven hundred."

"And how many cost $20?"

"Two. Did you want a room?"

"Sure." And I handed over my credit card and the clerk rang it up for $60. For the second time in two days, I went inside and lay on the bed with the air conditioner blasting away.

*

The heat was ridiculous in Vegas. I'd planned to ride all around Nevada, looking for Area 51 and doubling back up to the Loneliest Highway that runs through the middle of the state, but to hell with that—the next morning I took the direct route that crosses quickly over the baking scrub into Utah. There was no pleasure in fighting the heat, and it was just an endurance run on the interstate to St. George, Utah. There was a state welcome centre and I pulled in for a drink of water, but the centre was closed. "Back in 15 minutes," said the sign.

I'd wanted to go in and ask about the roads in the region, because I could see two choices: straight up the interstate to Salt Lake City, then into Colorado and higher ground, or straight east from St. George onto some squiggly lines on the map, ending up in Colorado's south. With nobody to ask, I sat beneath a shade tree next to my bike and pulled out the map again. I wanted to head for the squiggly lines, but if the road stayed low it would stay hot and take twice as long to get up into the cool mountains. I'd just decided to leave and boot it to Salt Lake when a woman walked by, and she paused to say hello.

"Are you from Ontario?" she asked. She'd seen the bike's license plate.

"Yes," I said, irritated.

"Oh—I'm from Ontario," she replied brightly, but I just grunted. Ten million people are from Ontario.

"Where are you from in Ontario?" she persisted, and I looked up at her with dull eyes and obvious disdain.

"Toronto," I said. "Well, near Toronto."

"Oh—I'm from near Toronto," she said with barely a pause. "Where are you from that's near Toronto?"

"Milton," I said, and hoped that would be the end of it.

"Oh—I'm from Milton," she said. "Whereabouts in Milton?"

And it turned out that Wilma and her husband Pete, who was waiting in their car in the parking lot, lived just three blocks from my home. It also turned out that they were on a fly/drive vacation arranged by their son, who worked for Air Canada and had a baggage allowance that let them take heavy bags on their flight at no charge. And they were a lovely couple.

They gave me a bottle of cool water and I gave them my bag with the tent and shock absorber, and some other stuff that wasn't really needed. They took it happily and I collected it all safely the following month.

*

Once I'd loaded my heavy bag into Wilma and Pete's car, the welcome centre had reopened. I went in to ask about the squiggly lines. "Ah, that's Hwy. 12 out of Zion National Park to Escalante," said the tourist adviser. "It goes straight up into the mountains and you'll be 30 degrees cooler up there. And it's one of *Car and Driver*'s 10 best roads in America—great on a motorcycle."

I fired the still-hot bike to life, headed for the squiggly lines and never looked back.

*

The ride across southern Utah was wonderful. The bike handled far better for having lost the heavy bag, and the temperature was ideal. The roads dipped and doodled around the low mountains and my mood rose with the altitude. At last, this was the road trip I was hoping for: Highway 9 through Zion, with its towers and monuments, then up to Highway 12 with its swooping esses and switchback zeds, and even a stretch known as the Hogsback that rides right on the spine of the mesa, with 1,000-foot drops to each side.

But this story isn't about the beauty of the road trip—there are enough others to tell those tales. It's about another look at the map once I made it to Colorado, when I saw another squiggly line outside Denver that had a piece of type pointing to it, which said "Highest Road in America." It was the road to Mount Evans, which is paved to the very top of the peak at 14,230 feet. It's more than 100 feet higher than Pike's Peak off to the south. How could I not go there?

In fact, the ride to the peak—the fifth-highest in all of Colorado—was relatively straightforward. The weather was perfect and I rode slowly and carefully and just kept slogging upwards. The road started out through trees, came out near a lake, and then passed above the treeline to rolling grassland; the last few thousand feet were switchbacked and very steep. My old carburetted motorbike coughed a bit from the altitude but kept on going all the way to the top. There's an old burned-down stone restaurant there (this is America, don't forget) and a parking lot and a short scramble to the absolute peak of the mountain. I took the GPS from the bike to carry its altimeter and stood on the marker of the peak and felt like a god—albeit a god who'd just twisted the throttle to get there. Then I climbed down again and coasted back down the mountain, careful not to ride the brakes.

In less than a week, I'd travelled from America's lowest road to its highest, and that really felt like an accomplishment, although the achievement belonged to the bike rather than myself. But the euphoria of Highway 12 was fading and the bike was starting to sag again. The brakes were wearing down and the turn signals weren't working properly. It would be at least a week to get home. I started wondering if she would make it.

We weren't quite finished, though. I wanted to ride around Rocky Mountain National Park before leaving, so I stayed in the high ground just north of Mount Evans and set off into the park the next day. The road quickly climbs above 10,000 feet—above the treeline—and once again, the weather was clear and warm. Traffic was fairly light and a few large animals wandered back and forth across the road. I had a good time and then it was time to leave.

I followed the loop out of the park and down from the mountains, heading east. I knew I'd not return for some while, and probably—hopefully—never on this motorcycle. As I rode down to the prairie, though, I was watching the bike's small speedometer, because the odometer was about to turn to 88,888.8 kilometres. As soon as it turned, I wanted to pull over for a photo. I'm a guy. It's what guys do.

As I looked across at the GPS on the handlebar as the 8s rolled into place, the altimeter showed my height. At that exact moment on the steep descent, it showed 8,888 feet.

There's no reason to this. It's just a coincidence. It means nothing, except it means everything. In Asia, eight is the luckiest number, and the more eights, the better. On this trip home, as I wondered if I'd make it and was dropping from the mountains to reality, my bike showed me all the eights—all of them. I knew it would be okay.

The next day, the speedometer broke and with it, the odometer. I relied on the GPS to know my distance and when to stop for gas. The front brake pads faded against the thinning disc, and the replacement shock absorber began leaking fluid. The headlight worked only on high beam, so I tipped the lamp down a little and carried on. And after a week we made it, all the way home, safely and intact, just as the eights promised. I knew we would.

Mark Richardson is the editor of Canada Moto Guide *and he loves a good road trip.* He is the author of Zen and Now: On the Trail of Robert Pirsig and the Art of Motorcycle Maintenance, *for which he rode his old motorcycle across the United States to California. In 2012, he drove a new Chevy Camaro convertible along the entire 7,600-kilometre length of the Trans-Canada Highway and the journey became his second book,* Canada's Road: A Journey on the Trans-Canada Highway from St. John's to Victoria.

🌐 *ZenAndNow.org*
🐦 *@WheelsMark*

EXTREME HEAT, AND GETTING IT WRONG

By Simon Thomas

It's 55°C (131°F). We're riding our loaded GS bikes at walking pace and the heat that's washing over me from my engine, which is running at 170°C (338°F), is horrendous. I feel like a boil-in-the-bag-chicken. Christ, just breathing feels like I'm sipping air from a furnace.

In Senegal's southeast corner we've been riding a stony cattle track through bush scrub for two days. Our crawling pace has gained us just 69 miles. We left Kédougdu with 40 litres of water; we have four litres remaining. We're exhausted and my mouth feels like a bag of ass covered in dust.

Up ahead my wife Lisa is struggling as the front wheel of her F650GS is snatched hard to the right, bouncing off the coarse red rock of our laterite track. Both our bikes are fully fuelled, which is more than can be said for their riders.

Yesterday had been tough and we'd hoped that today wasn't going to be worse. Satadougou village sits just inside Mali and only five kilometres from where we'd camped last night. We'd pick up water there.

Was it the heat, dehydration, our inexperience, stupidity, or had we just misread the map? Squeezing the brakes we pull to a stop, past a thicket of sandy scrub. My jaw's on the tank and a knot of panic launches from my gut into my mouth. Neither Lisa nor I had interpreted the meandering line of demarcation separating Senegal and Mali as a river (Mistake 1), which it most definitely is.

As we walk the banks of the Faléme River, it's obvious there's nowhere shallow enough for us to ford it. "Well, there's no sodding way I'm riding back the way we came," Lisa states adamantly.

At the bottom of the steep riverbank, an ancient pirogue (dug-out canoe) rests at the water's edge. "Well, there's no way our bikes will fit in that" I blurt, as I hopefully look to Lisa for reassurance. "There's got be another way across...right?"

"I have a boat, it's okay for one ton!" exclaims the pirogue owner triumphantly, in heavily accented African French.

"That's not a boat," I murmur flatly. "It's a hollowed-out tree trunk."

With no miracle solution in sight, it's decision time. Either ride back or grow a set, load the bikes, and trust that this guy can get them across.

With the help of four local men from Satadougou, we load the bikes and precariously paddle them across. On the far side we pay $2 USD, three crumpled cigarettes, and a BMW key fob. I take a long, slow, hot breath of relief, my first in the two and a half hours the process has taken. The 10 litres of river water we've siphoned into our water bags will get us to the small village of Kéniéba just 50 kilometres farther north. (Mistake 2.)

As we enter Satadougou, Lisa's F650GS exhaust note cracks the air like a machine gun; as if on cue Satadougou erupts in a rehearsed siege of collective excitement and euphoria. Entire families launch themselves from the dark shelter of their twig and mud homes and charge us with hands outstretched. I'm awkwardly aware of the glaring contrast between our loud and high-tech appearance versus the National Geographic centrefold we've just ridden into. Like conquering heroes, we're chased to the village centre to frenzied cries of "cadeau, cadeau" (gift, gift). Everyone here thinks we're part of the Dakar rally which occasionally passes through. My shallow little man-ego can't find reason enough to tell them otherwise and we exit the village a little taller than when we'd entered.

By early afternoon, the warm smiles of Satadougou seem a million miles away. The track has narrowed, the rocks seem to be breeding, the heat is debilitating, and I'm learning to hate my GPS, which is now just a reminder of exactly how little distance we've covered. We've crossed half a dozen dry riverbeds and negotiated countless very steep gullies. My concentration is waning and my balance is faltering.

When we stop to stretch our now-cramping calves, Lisa, her head bowed, whispers, "Why didn't we soak ourselves and our riding kit in the river to cool down?"

"I didn't even think about that," I confess, shaking my head, suddenly ashamed not to have recognised this now obvious cooling opportunity (Mistake 3). Amidst a sea of sun-blonde tall grass, there is no shade.

We guzzle our water, not for a second thinking about keeping a reserve. Kéniéba is a mere 30 kilometres farther north; we'll be there by afternoon. (Mistake 4.)

My lips are parched, the water's gone and my mouth is drier than a dead dingo's donger, to quote an Aussie mate. My brain's having a hard time processing the best route around the deep channels that were cut into the red ground during the rainy season. Lisa's already picked herself up after three slow but heavy spills. She's not saying much.

Exhaustion is setting in and my hamstrings threaten to cramp each time I need to stand on the pegs. We've thought about stopping to camp, but small bush fires are popping up and the thought of burning to death in our tent whilst we sleep isn't really working for us!

Feeling like a pair of beaten desert donkeys, we roll into Kéniéba in the late afternoon and for 5,000 CFA (£6) find a room with a dirty mattress on a concrete floor. In a small straw-roofed courtyard, I sip a warm Coke, and with heavy eyelids I begin to relax. Without warning, my legs tighten and I'm gripped in a vice-like pain as every sinew in both my legs spasms and contracts so violently I'm panicked. Lost for breath, I can barely yelp. Two men sat close by hoist me violently upward, one under each armpit, until my stagger becomes a walk and the cramps finally subside. These are the worst cramps I've ever experienced. Lisa and I have drunk two full glasses of water mixed with tablespoons of salt. In the corner of the dusty room, our once-black riding jackets are powder-white and standing rigid upright on the floor. We've both lost so much salt through sweat that we've crystallised our riding gear. I didn't know that was possible.

*

Today we started late; it took half the day just to rehydrate (Mistake 5). We're north of Kéniéba. The horizon's been nothing more than a melting, shimmering blur all day. The heat's unrelenting. It's 6 pm and we're wobbling along a narrow track, squeezing our bikes between thickets of barbed thorny bushes. The 45 litres of water we're carrying mean we've got an extra 45 kilos to deal with. We've downed 15 litres each today, neither of us needs to piss, our throats are parched, and we've stopped sweating. We've got to camp now and sleep.

I can't remember what it's like to be cool. It's taken hours to make a just a few kilometres and the water's getting low, again! At the bottom of a steep escarpment we find dappled shade under a lone acacia bush. Once again, it's decision time. To our east, we can see the quickly rising narrow track that we'll need to take to reach the village of Kassama. As exhausted and dehydrated as we are, it looks like a clusterfuck waiting to happen, and we've already got a ton of "shit-creek" action going on. I've got the energy of a wind-caught plastic bag and I don't want to do this anymore. Our once-dreamy bike adventure is baring its teeth.

"We can't risk getting stuck in those mountains," Lisa finally babbles. I grunt in agreement. We'll head north to Bafoulabé. For Christ's sake, it's only 56 miles as the crow flies. By the side of the track, I watch, helpless, as Lisa, unable to think coherently, sits on her bike, kills the ignition, drops her head, and cries. We've got to keep going!

*

We made the decision to head north two days ago. On the outskirts of Bafoulabé, the smooth tar under our wheels feels strange, like the quiet before a storm. Without a village or a well in sight, we'd run out of water and resorted to drinking the brine from the cans of vegetables we were carrying. Cramps, nausea, and hallucinations hadn't been included in our dreams of adventure.

Yesterday I'd stared blankly as I watched Santa Claus, complete with his team of reindeer, pull right past me on the track. Real enough to touch? Sure. Last night, Lisa mentioned she'd watched the odometer of her 650 run backwards whilst she sat stationary on her bike.

Our kidneys ache like they've been hammered by Mike Tyson. We're lucky to have reached here and we know it. It's taken us four days to ride 189 kilometres.

As we sit in a small café in town, never has a rusting ceiling fan and cold Coke looked so good.

Simon and Lisa Thomas are considered by many to be the world's foremost adventure motorcyclists, with more "real-world" experience than anyone on the road today.

Lisa and Simon helped define what is now called "adventure riding." Since setting out on their journey in 2003, the duo has amassed an insane 500,000 miles on their ride, through 81 countries on six continents. Along the way they've traversed 36 deserts, survived a broken neck in the Amazon jungle, cheated death, and are still travelling today.

This pair of explorers, writers, photographers, and public speakers inspires adventure. Find out more at: www.2RidetheWorld

🌐 *2RideTheWorld.com*

/2RideTheWorld

📷 *@2RideTheWorld*

/2RideTheWorld

WHERE ARE WE?

By Michelle Lamphere

After fueling up in the last small town, I check my map again before leading us east in search of a turn onto a dirt road that will lead us back into the mountains. We've already burned through half our allotment of daylight today, but we've made good progress under the clear blue autumn sky.

Ten miles ahead, the gravel road stretches out across a high desert plain, dry golden land running as far as I can see to the base of the mountains in the distance. Scrubby brush covers the ground, and is likely the only thing holding down the sandy soil in this steady breeze.

I tick off landmarks from my mental checklist as we cross one creek, and then another, and take lefts and rights at various forks in the road, but we finally run off the edge of my memorized portion of the map. As I roll my XT250 to a stop to memorize the next section, Molly pulls up beside me and acknowledges the beauty of the countryside. There won't be any more turns for the next 15 to 20 miles, so she rides on as I take a photo of her and her dusty trail in front of a backdrop of slate-gray mountains. I wave Tammy ahead, too, and grab a shot of my companions riding into the distance.

Motorcycles brought us together, as they do for so many people, but our friendship was forged from unfortunate events. Lemonade from lemons. Molly was riding the Trans-Labrador Highway on her TW200 a few years ago, and stopped in Newfoundland for some fresh ink to celebrate the occasion. While she was inside the tattoo shop, her bike was stolen, something virtually unheard of in that land of endless generosity. Molly reported the theft to a St. John's radio station and a group of local riders, including Tammy, came to her rescue, eventually getting her bike back to Molly.

A couple of years after that, I wrecked my bike on the Trans-Labrador Highway and broke my leg. After being flown to Newfoundland for surgery, I found myself in need of a place to stay. A local rider forum connected me with Tammy, who came to my rescue as well. She took me and my boyfriend in for three months before I could continue my journey. Tammy is the common link between us, our heroine.

Rolling hills offer glimpses of the girls as they leapfrog each other, taking turns to stop for photos now and then as we near the base of the spine of the continent. Tammy rides her KL250 off the edge of the road and parks as Molly putters on. We are each lost in the gorgeous day and landscape. I stop to watch sheep grazing on the open range guarded by a half-dozen enormous white dogs. Bells clang softly among the sheep as they wander and graze.

Over the next rise I spot Molly parked at a rutted trail, waiting for Tammy and me to catch up. In the distance, she has spotted a small camp perched on a knoll above the grazing herd of more than a thousand head of sheep. Molly points to it and wonders aloud if we should stop. There's a small trailer with two horses tethered to it and a tin-covered sheepherder's wagon, something I haven't seen in decades. My grandparents lived in one in western South Dakota when they were first married, more than 60 years ago, and my grandfather spent a few summers watching over a small herd from the window of their tiny home. Sheep-wagons have gone the way of the dinosaur in my part of the world, and it would be a real treat to see one.

Molly leads us off the road along the bumpy trail before deciding to ride over a berm, out onto the hillside, aiming directly for the camp. Tammy and I follow. Not wanting to spook the horses, we stop fifty yards short of camp and shut off our bikes. As I tug at my chin strap and hang my helmet on my bars, a small Peruvian man steps out of the back of the wagon and gives us the once-over. I wave and call out to put his mind at ease, "Hola, amigo. Buenos días."

The fine features of his face relax immediately as he waves back. I walk over to make introductions and translate for the girls. I explain that we are friends, and are travelling together along the spine of the continent, making our way south. Tammy and Molly will be on the road for a few months. I am only able to travel with them for a short portion of the ride, but am happy to be here in this beautiful place. I explain that I've always wanted to see a working sheep-wagon because my grandparents used to live in one. This makes our new friend smile and he beckons us toward his home while he darts inside to quickly tidy up.

Hernado, our involuntary host, waves to invite us inside, warning each of us to mind the hot woodstove just inside the door as we enter. Molly and Tammy take turns before I climb the wooden ladder and step into a live version of my childhood dream. Inside, everything is painted a soft mint green, from the floor to the arching ceiling overhead and everything in between. I sit on a built-in wooden bench and admire the small, neatly made bunk, the sparse shelves burdened only with a single set of dining utensils, a heavy raincoat hanging on a hook by the bed, and the incredible view behind me through the door I entered. Sort of like a hard-top version of covered wagons, this must have been the original RV. It's quaint and cute, just enough. I don't want to invade his privacy for long and thank him for the tour as I step back outside.

Hernado introduces us to his horses, which are named the color of their respective coats, Rojito and Blanco, and tells us about the dogs guarding his sheep. Two of the dogs must be off duty, as they're sleeping in the shade under the wagon. He works for a wealthy man who owns the herd and who brought Hernado and the wagons here two months back. He will stay another month before the owner comes to retrieve him. I ask about food and supplies, and he says that he was delivered to camp with everything he needed for a summer in the mountains.

Molly speaks freely in English, knowing that our new friend can't understand our open conversation. I'd planned to make our trio a curry for supper that night with a few vegetables that I'd packed safely away in my panniers for a special meal. We normally just snack during the riding day and have dinner once we settle into camp, but Molly wonders if we could make the curry for lunch instead and share it with Hernado. Tammy and I love the idea.

After retrieving my backpacker stove from my bike, I set to work with my tiny cook set to make a meal for four. Hernado offers to contribute as well, but we insist it will be our pleasure because he has been so gracious in welcoming three foreign strangers into his camp. Molly, Tammy and I each only travel with a single cookpot which doubles as a bowl, so I'm grateful Hernado has his own plate.

Tammy offers moose jerky from Newfoundland as an appetizer while I work on lunch. Boiled water revives a dehydrated curry meal for two and warms a packet of Indian lentils that I stretch with the aid of a diced zucchini. Hot beverages and fresh slices of tomato complete the menu. It's not much, but it's not bad.

Our Peruvian host tells us a little about himself. He misses his wife and children but is happy to have work, even if it's far from home. We ask several questions while I try my best to translate both sides of the conversation. I apologize for my Spanish being a little slow, but I'm grateful that we seem to easily understand each other. He is from Huancayo, a hundred miles east of Lima. I tell him that while I haven't been to Huancayo, I have travelled by motorcycle to many other places in Peru on my southward journey to Ushuaia. I tell him I love every part of his country, but mostly its beautiful people. He smiles.

Somewhere along the way we find out that he played in a band. When I ask which instrument, he says, surprising me, that he plays the saxophone. Molly has me ask if he has it with him, and he does. Perhaps being a bit too forward, I take a chance, and ask if he will play something for us. He obliges and goes inside to retrieve his shiny Italian sax to entertain us, his gift in exchange for a small plate of rehydrated foreign food.

The afternoon sun has warmed the land and the stronger breeze of the morning has relaxed into a mellowed drift. My friends and I each find a place to stretch out between scrubby brush on the flat space between our bikes and the wagon while Hernado plays a melancholy Peruvian tune. I hold my breath, listening intently, and take pause to notice every detail of the moment, something I do when I want to preserve it for later. My mind lingers on every note, listening to each drift into the distance on a gentle east-bound wind.

When he finishes, we clap, and thank him. I don't want the moment to end, but the day is moving on and so should we. But thankfully, Hernado starts another tune, allowing this dreamlike bubble to hold its fragile shape a moment longer. The notes of the song are soothing, subtle, and muted as only a saxophone can make. Sheep graze, drifting east with the breeze, along the rugged land while the dogs doze around the perimeter of the herd in the sun. From our vantage point on the knoll we seem to have more than 180 degrees of view between the western and eastern horizons. Snow-capped mountains watch over us from the north, while the desert beckons not far south. In a moment, Hernado finishes the song.

We each find some food in our panniers to offer him for his hospitality. I make gifts of a banana and a slightly dented apple, as well as some oatmeal and chocolate-covered almonds. Tammy leaves her highly prized moose jerky and Molly finds some dried fruit, oatmeal, and other goodies to share. We pack away our gear, give hugs to our new friend, and thank him for a wonderful afternoon.

There's a lot of miles to cover before we reach the river where we hope to camp tonight. As I put on my helmet and gloves, I look around, reminding myself I've been in Wyoming all day, not Peru, riding south on the Continental Divide Route. You never know who or what you'll find around the next corner on a motorcycle journey, perhaps even a saxophone-playing Peruvian sheepherder in the middle of the Rocky Mountains.

Michelle Lamphere is a self-professed travel addict and writer. She grew up in Sturgis, South Dakota, home to one of the most famous motorcycle rallies in the world, but didn't start riding until she was 30.

In 2013 Michelle quit her 21-year executive career, sold her home, and hit the road for Ushuaia, Argentina (via Newfoundland). What started out as an extended vacation and break between careers turned into a two-year journey from South Dakota to South America across 20 countries and 45,000 miles.

In September 2015 she published Tips for Travelling Overland in Latin America, *and in 2017 she published* The Butterfly Route, *her memoir from her two-year journey.*

Each year she spends as much time as possible happily travelling the world, and often finds herself not wanting to go home.

🌐 *SturgisChick.com*

🐦 *@SturgisChick*

📷 *@SturgisChick*

NO, ACTUALLY, IT S THE DESTINATION

By Jeremy Kroeker

One of the great joys of riding a Kawasaki KLR 650 is making fun of people who ride BMWs. "You paid what, for what? My bike, *with luggage*, cost what you just paid to change your spark plugs!" The trusty KLR, everyone agrees, has deficiencies (it's ugly, slow, underpowered, spews smoke, sounds like you put gravel in the oil pan instead of oil ... I could go on), but it always gets you there. Always. Besides, if it does break down, you don't need a laptop to fix it, *wink, nudge.*

And so, when my KLR broke down in Calgary this summer, and my girlfriend arrived on her BMW F700GS to tow me to the nearest mechanic (using a length of pink paracord), I found myself rather reticent. Elle didn't say much either, but she had a spring in her step and she wanted a lot of photos that day.

A week later the old KLR struggled to start when I picked it up from the shop, but it sounded okay after warming up. Was that a little sputter? No. I'm sure it's fine.

To mitigate the risk of another breakdown I chose to test the bike in a controlled environment, setting off with Elle on a ten-day tour of remote gravel roads through the Canadian Rockies.

"I'll bring some paracord," said Elle.

"And don't forget your laptop," I wanted to say, but I just gritted my teeth instead.

Yeah, remote gravel roads on newly repaired machinery may not seem like a brilliant idea, but I'm not really known for good ideas. Anyway, it's a KLR. It'll always get you where you want to go. Always.

The bikes hummed over Highwood Pass, a smooth strip of pavement that climbs southeast from the Trans-Canada Highway through Kananaskis Country, Alberta, to an elevation just below the treeline, and where pockets of snow often survive the brief summer. Carrying my camping gear, and at these elevations, the only thing that changes on my bike when I crack open the throttle is the sound of the engine. With it absolutely pinned, I could just barely maintain the speed limit. Elle, astride her BMW, didn't notice any elevation gain except for the scenery. I could see her in my mirrors, her fake red ponytail atop her silver helmet flapping in the summer breeze.

Finally my engine gasped with relief as we topped out and began a gentle decline toward Longview, Alberta. We stopped at a lonely gas station along the way, just as the girl was locking up. She stuck around to let us fuel before leaving us in the golden light of a warm Alberta evening.

We watched hummingbirds flit about as we took a little time to stretch and have a snack. From here, we planned to ride just over 100 kilometres south along the gravel forestry trunk road, Highway 940, to Coleman, Alberta, near the boundary of British

Columbia. Besides struggling in the thin air of a high mountain pass, which was normal, my KLR seemed fine.

"We should be in Coleman in a couple of hours," I said, staring down the road. All summer, smoke from vast forest fires in BC and Alberta had tinged the mountain air a dusty orange, and this evening was just the same.

Elle is a capable rider, having twice ridden from Canada to Panama, and once up to the Arctic Circle in Alaska, but she prefers hard pack to loose gravel. She'll never complain, and she'll never back down, but she rides at her own pace, standing on her pegs.

"There are several exit points on this road that could take us to pavement," I assured her. But, really, I was just making myself feel better. I had ridden this stretch before. For a gravel road, it's well maintained. It winds through the foothills and Rocky Mountains of southern Alberta. It's just that I still had a bad feeling about the reliability of my old bike.

"And anyway," I added, clearly for my own benefit, "we have all our camping gear with us. So, if we run out of time, we can just find a place to spend the night."

I shot off down the road ahead of Elle, tracing a squiggly line with my back tire as the KLR pulled hard through the dust. Funny. My bike is cumbersome and slow on the highway, but I could still travel at about 100 kilometres per hour in these conditions and it felt fine. I just had to pick my line, stick to the wheel ruts of all the trucks that had gone before.

Soon I had the road to myself. I knew that Elle wouldn't mind. Whereas my riding style caused many, "Oh, crap!" moments, whenever I pulled over to thank my lucky sprockets, I'd soon see Elle, steadfastly trundling along, standing on her pegs, red ponytail slapping off her silver helmet.

Then I'd shoot off again. "Oh, crap!" Etc.

I relaxed my pace as I approached a bridge over a clear mountain stream. This would make a nice spot to pull over and click of a photo of Elle, I thought. As I squeezed in my clutch and coasted to a stop, my engine sputtered and cut out, but when I pressed the starter, it fired right back up to a smooth idle. I never took the photo, as the little engine failure distracted me. When Elle came rolling by I gave her the all-clear sign. She carried on and I soon caught up and passed her.

Now and then, even at speed, I'd depress the clutch to see what the engine would do. Sometimes it held, and sometimes it stalled. And it seemed to be getting worse. It began to sputter like I had the choke on. When I had broken down in Calgary, it seemed like a fuel problem. I knew that my petcock didn't work properly—it didn't portion out reserve fuel—so, like a Neanderthal mechanic, I simply dropped the bike on its left side to splash extra gas where it needed to go. That often works if the bike is truly low on fuel. (It's also a great excuse if you tip over in a parking lot. "What are you laughing at? I did that on purpose. I'm just out of gas.")

That hadn't solved the problem. Next I removed the seat and gas tank, unscrewed the sparkplug, grounded it, and checked for spark. Yep. All good. The plug looked old, and markings on it belied a lean air/fuel mixture, but otherwise it seemed fine. I happened to be carrying a spare plug, so I changed it anyway.

After that, the bike ran fine ... for about 20 minutes. Enter Elle with her pink paracord and a humiliating tow to the mechanic, foot peg to foot peg. The shop diagnosed the problem as a faulty spark lead and, after patching it up (no, not replacing it), they declared the bike mechanically sound.

Yet here we were, sputtering down a gravel road. We stopped at the first exit point. A short gravel ride east would lead us to the pavement of the "Cowboy Trail," Highway 22. Conveniently, the little spur would kick us out very near the acreage where Elle's parents live, and we could reconsider our options there.

Then again, just as we pulled up to the junction, my bike decided to behave.

"It's running fine now," I shouted to Elle over the engines. "We're probably about half-way to Coleman," (we were not) "and besides, there's another exit point farther south if we need it. Might just have been some bad gas that worked its way through." (It was not. And also, is it ever? No.)

We opted to continue south toward Coleman. All along the way, it was a case of sputtering performance punctuated by bewildering moments of perfect functionality. Again, arriving at the nominally safer option of a short retreat east to pavement, we carried on south.

We rode past a firebase bustling with firefighters in yellow coveralls. There were heavy-duty diesel trucks idling by the road, and cumbersome Bell 212 helicopters and the like, their rotors spinning to a slow halt as they shut down for the evening. I had lived and worked at this base over a decade ago, but I was too distracted by the situation to indulge in nostalgia. All I wanted was to arrive in Coleman before dark, find a place to sleep, and figure out what to do in the morning.

More sputtering, faltering, and stalling ensued, but I did eventually reach the destination. I landed ahead of Elle because, in moments where my bike seemed fine, I sped like mad in a race against the setting sun. When I arrived in town, I pulled in the clutch near a graveyard and, fittingly, the bike died. Soon after, Elle came lumbering along. The red ponytail on her helmet was, like me, limp, lifeless, ready for this day to wind down into a peaceful night.

The next day could have broken us ... the relationship between me and Elle, the relationship between me and my KLR. Take your pick. But Elle played it perfect. She was neither obsequious, nor indignant, nor abrupt. She was a parts runner, sounding board, sympathetic observer, and consultant. She seemed happy and content, but not exultant because my bike had failed and hers had not. In other words, she kept things in perspective. We were safe. We were dry. We lived in Canada. And we had been slightly delayed on our motorcycle vacation. Are you complaining? And, if so, why?

After trying various fixes, including fuel additives and pulling the bike apart right down to the various components of the carburetor, I admitted defeat. In hindsight, it was probably the patched up sparkplug lead after all. Also, somewhere along the way, a breather tube had been misrouted from the gas tank to the carburetor. I had definitely done it the last time, just mindlessly putting things back where I had found them, but who did it first? Who knows, but I sure didn't notice the error in Coleman.

Elle called her father, who arrived a few hours later with his little pickup truck to rescue us. After loading the KLR, we retired to the local pub where I had a few pints to ... well, there's no reason for it. I just had a bunch of drinks.

By then it was twilight. We geared up after dinner, Elle doubling me back to her parent's acreage, her red ponytail slapping me in the face as we went. With several pints in me (and a few shots) I may not have been the ideal passenger. I made inappropriate stabs at the controls on Elle's bike, and at Elle herself. Maybe I grabbed her helmet and shook it a few times. I can't remember. But there are photos on my phone that suggest that I should probably apologize to this long-suffering girl.

We arrived at Elle's parents' house after dark. We made arrangements to drive the truck with my KLR to my friend's house in Bragg Creek. He could fix the bike, he reassured us. In the meantime, we'd drive to Canmore, Alberta, where the journey originally began. There, we'd pick up my other motorcycle, drive back to Elle's parent's place for her bike, and continue on our journey to BC.

Fortunately, I had a spare motorcycle. The next morning it started right up. That's the great thing about a 1982 Honda CB750 Custom—it might not be pretty, but it always gets you there. Always.

Jeremy Kroeker is the author of Motorcycle Therapy, and Through Dust and Darkness.

- 🌐 *MotorcycleTherapy.com*
- 🐦 *@Jeremy_Kroeker*
- 📷 *@Jeremy_Kroeker*
- 📷 *@MotorcycleTherapy*
- 📘 */OscillatorPress*

AFTERWORD

Good grief. In the first *Motorcycle Messengers,* I actually wrote these words, "At the end of every book project, I silently promise myself that I'll never do *that* again." Never do another book project, I say.

And yet, here we are.

It's just that, the more I travel to motorcycle shows and events to promote my own books, the more I meet interesting people who have amazing stories to tell. Many of them have written books that you, dear reader, may not know about. And you must!

As Charley Boorman writes in the foreword, reading about grand adventures is inspiring. No, you may not clutch a machete in your teeth and embark on a ten-year odyssey through the Pantanal, but reading about Lois Pryce and her journey through Iran may give you the idea that you might like to have your own adventure.

That's cool.

Anything can be an adventure with the right attitude, and taking off on a motorcycle is a step in the right direction. It's good to explore. It's good to challenge your own beliefs with an open mind and heart. And, very often, when you cross a cultural boundary, you discover that we are all just citizens of earth with more in common than not. That's comforting.

By the way, it's best to discover that from the saddle of a motor-cycle. Any bike will do.

Jeremy Kroeker
Alberta, Canada
2018

ACKNOWLEDGEMENTS

Oscillator Press acknowledges no one.

Just kidding. It's just that we're tempted to omit this section because it's so difficult to write without listing thousands of people. But here goes ...

We are thankful to each and every contributor—even the many fine writers who sent us stories that we didn't use. We are especially thankful to those who submitted their material on deadline as we fumbled to meet our own. Here we must mention, once again, Sam Manicom. A friend. A professional. Thank you.

Of course, thanks to Charley Boorman for giving of his time and effort to write a thoughtful foreword, and to his friend, Billy Ward, for helping to facilitate everything. At Oscillator Press, we're fans of your work, Charley. Thanks for lending a hand.

Once again, Scott Manktelow designed the cover and, again, had to be dragged out of retirement to do it. He's in the early stages of his medical practice now, so he does not need the work. In fact, he doesn't even have time for this work, which is why we're so glad he took the project.

Jennifer Groundwater did a great job of copyediting. Then the staff at Oscillator Press took her work and inserted errors. She fixed those errors, and we inserted more. If there's a problem, it's because of us, not Jennifer. If you need editing done, look to her.

Rosie Gabrielle provided the photos for the front and back covers. She's been through a lot, as you can see by her YouTube channel, *YouTube.com/RosieGabrielle*.

Lin Oosterhoff did a great job with layout of text. Thank you.

We're not sure if Dan Sparks wanted his contribution to this project to remain anonymous or not, so we'll just thank him for unspecified support. He is generous.

And then, there are the friends, supporters, and fans of Oscillator Press. No, we can't list you all. It's a bit of a copout to say, "You know who you are," but we don't know what else to say.

OK. OK. Here's a partial list:

Elle West talked us down from many ledges and stopped us from hitting "delete" so many times. Bryan Bayley is weird, and we like him. He's also a caring, generous, and insightful friend. Nevil Stow still makes the best margarita north of El Paso. Dave Coe is the best campfire guitar player we know, and he's always supportive. Paddy Tyson from *Overland Magazine* is a champion of motorcycle travel writing. Thank you. Mark Richardson from *CanadaMotoGuide.com* is a great writer, a patient editor, and a friend. We've tested the limits of his patience recently, but we hope that sharing a wee dram with him one day will make things right. Speaking of *CanadaMotoGuide.com,* thank you, Rob Harris. We miss you.

We won't list more people because where do you stop? But we will say this: thank you, Ted Simon. With your writing, you have inspired so many.

Now, let's go for a rip!

ALSO BY JEREMY KROEKER.

From the Canadian Rockies to Panamanian jungle, Motorcycle Therapy rumbles with comic adventure as two men, fleeing failed relationships, test the limits of their motorcycles and their friendship. Join the horn-honking, signal-flashing, wheelie-popping pair as they endure painful bee stings, painful snakebites and 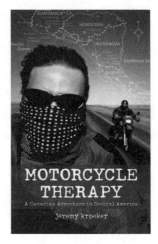 (when they talk to girls) painful humiliation. Even if you hate reading, motorcycles and travel books, you'll love reading this motorcycle travel book.

"With humour that's reminiscent of Bill Bryson's best, Kroeker discovers that you can't leave yourself behind – but it's sure fun trying."

Chris Scott, author of *Adventure Motorcycling Handbook*.

JEREMY KROEKER is a Mennonite with a motorcycle. When his seemingly unflinching faith in a Christian worldview begins to shift, he hops on his bike to seek answers. After shipping his ride to Europe, Kroeker discovers that the machine wobbles worse than his own opinions about spirituality. Still, he caries on, oscillating

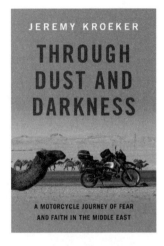

through Germany, Austria, Croatia, Albania, and into the Middle East: Turkey, Syria, Lebanon and, ultimately the theocratic nation of Iran.

It is there that Kroeker takes a forbidden visit to a holy Muslim Shrine. Once inside, invisible hands rip from his heart a sincere prayer, his first in many years. And God hears that prayer. For before Kroeker can escape Iran, God steals into his hotel room one night to threaten him with death. At least, that's one way to look at it.

Oscillator Press thanks the following sponsors.

MOTOLOGY SCHOOL

Motology School is licensed by Alberta Transportation and is approved by Honda Learn to Ride School. Located in Calgary, our mission is to provide a premium, safe, and fun environment

for our students in a well-organized setting. Come learn to ride with us and gain the skills you need for the road.

- ⊕ MotologySchool.com
- ✉ Info@motologyschool.com
- ✆ 403.909.6686
- ▪ /MotologySchool
- ▣ @motology_school

MOTOLOMBIA

Motolombia has been running soul-inspiring motorcycle tours and offering rentals in South America since 2008. Some 40+ adventure-ready motorcycles are waiting for you to realize your "next top-of-the-bucket-list" destination - Colombia!

- ⊕ Motolombia.com
- ✉ booking@motolombia.com
- ▪ /motolombia
- ✆ @motolombia
- ▣ @motolombia
- ✆ +57 (2) 665 95 48
- ⌂ Cali, Colombia, South America

MOUNTAIN MEN MECHANICS

Mountain Men Mechanics will get you back up and running when you're in a jam. We're here for you 7-days a week. Get a mountain man on it!

- 🌐 MountainMenMechanics.com
- 📘 /mountainmenmechanics
- 🐦 @getamountainman
- 📷 @mountainmenmechanics
- ✉️ shop@mountainmenmechanics.com
- 📞 403.762.1678
- 🏠 141 Eagle Cres. Banff, Alberta

OVERLAND EXPO

The world's most unique event for do-it-yourself adventure travel enthusiasts, with 100s of classes, inspirational programs, roundtable discussions, demonstrations, food, and 300+ vendors.

- 🌐 OverlandExpo.com
- ✉️ info@overlandexpo.com
- 📷 @overlandexpo
- 🐦 @overlandexpo
- 📘 /overlandexpo

UNIVERSAL CYCLE SERVICES LTD.

Calgary's largest independent motorcycle shop. Specializing in KLR650's and offering service, parts & accessories for anything on two wheels. We have a Dyno machine for performance analysis, machine shop and ultra-sonic cleaning services. We are also the Canadian distributor of Drayko Jeans. Proudly serving motorcyclists since 1984!

- 🌐 UniversalCycle.ca
- ✉ general@universalcycle.ca
- 📞 403.277.0512
- 🏠 3924 – 3A Street NE, Calgary, Alberta, T2E 6R4

BLACKFOOT MOTOSPORTS

With over 50,000 square feet, we are your industry leading power sports dealership through knowledge, service, and customer satisfaction since 1970. One Team - One Plan - One Goal"

- 🌐 BlackfootOnline.com
- ✉ Sales@blackfootonline.com
- 📞 403.243.2636
- 🏠 6 Highfield Circle SE Calgary, Alberta T2G 5N5
- 📘 /blackfootonline
- 🐦 @blackfootonline
- 📷 @blackfootonline
- ▶ @blackfootonline

TOAD ROCK MOTORCYCLE CAMPGROUND

We especially love motorcycle campers, but everyone is welcome... even you!

📞 250.229.5448

🏠 2865 Toad Rock Road
on Highway 31
(Between Balfour, BC and Ainsworth, BC)
British Columbia, Canada

✉ information@toadrockcampground.com

Balfour, BC, Canada
www.toadrockcampground.com

WILD LIFE DISTILLERY

Wild Life Distillery produces premium sipping spirits in the heart of the Canadian Rockies. 100% Alberta grains are used to create beautiful, hand-crafted spirits.

Swing by the distillery for an amazing craft cocktail and a tour! (Open Weds-Sun tours at 3pm)

🌐 WildLifeDistillery.ca

🐦 @wldspirits

📷 @wldspirits

📘 /wldspirits

✉ info@wildlifedistillery.ca

📞 403.678.2800

🏠 160-105 Bow Meadows Crescent, Canmore, AB, T1W 2W8

PIKILILY

Empowering women and bringing safe motorcycling to African communities through grassroots training in road safety and motorcycle maintenance.

🌐 Pikilily.com
🐦 @pikilily_tz
📷 @pikilily_tz
📘 /pikilily
✉ info@pikilily.com
🏠 Mwanza, Tanzania, East Africa

OVERLAND MAGAZINE

OVERLAND Magazine, the quality international quarterly dedicated to motorcycle travel, contains captivating stories and stunning photography to inspire, enthuse and entertain.

🌐 OverlandMag.com
✉ editor@overlandmag.com
✉ sales@overlandmag.com
🏠 Box 726, Banbury OX16 6LY, UK

TRAIL TAIL

The most versatile single wheel motorcycle trailer around! Trail Tail thrives
on dirt, excels on pavement and provides cargo space to haul your gear
anywhere.

- 🌐 TrailTail.com
- ✉ fstolk@trailtail.com
- 📞 250.859.2467
- 📷 @trailtail
- 📘 /trailtail
- ▶ /channel/UCSrb_tIb0QG0GMgVeIZ7YxA
- 🏠 3D – 150 Campion Street
  Kelowna, BC, Canada V1X 7S8

SUMMIT MOTOSPORTS

Summit Motosports Sales, Service,
Parts, Accessories and Rentals. The
only licensed motorcycle shop in the
Bow Valley serving Canmore, Banff
and Lake Louise, Canada.

- 🌐 SummitMotosports.com
- 📷 @summitmotosports
- 🏠 104 - 109 Bow Meadows Crescent, Canmore, Alberta T1W 2W8
- 📞 403.609.2706
- ✉ Info@summitmotosports.com